A New Naturalism

Natural planting on the shingle beach near Dungeness Power Station, Kent, Summer 2002. Photo: Juliet Sargeant

A NEW NATURALISM

Catherine Heatherington

Juliet Sargeant

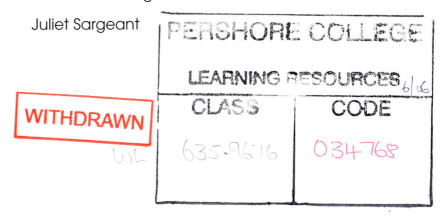

PACKARD PUBLISHING LIMITED

CHICHESTER

A New Naturalism
© 2005 Catherine Heatherington and Juliet Sargeant

First published by Packard Publishing Limited, Forum House, Stirling Road, Chichester, West Sussex, PO19 7DN, UK.

ISBN 1 85341 133 7

A CIP catalogue record for this book is available from the British Library.

Edited by Michael Packard.
Designed by Louise Burston. Layouts by Kate Barrett, Geoffrey Smith and Michael Packard.
Typeset by Dorwyn Limited, Wells, Somerset.
Printed in the United Kingdom by rpm print & design, Chichester, W. Sussex.

Acknowledgements

This book would not have been possible without the help of professional garden designers, researchers, horticulturalists, garden enthusiasts, friends and family. We would like to thank the following people:

Jill Billington for introducing us to the endless possibilities for planting design;

Nigel Dunnett for invaluable insights into the research and science behind the art of garden design;

Garden writer, Noël Kingsbury, for his encouragement and advice, with this, our first book;

Other designers for their generosity in sharing their ideas and working practices –
Lee Heykoop,
Piet Oudolf,
Dan Pearson,
Tim Rees,
Brita von Schoenaich,
Tom Stuart-Smith;

Gardeners, garden owners and horticulturalists for outlining the practical issues involved –
Mark Brown,
Ian Davies,
Judy Mahatane,
Bill Makins,
Mike Mullis,
Philip Oldham,
Judy and Malcolm Pearce;

Michael Packard whose inspiration led us to write this book;

Chris Sargeant and Larry Mindel for knowing when to agree and when to disagree.

Dedication

With thanks to Jill Billington

With love to Chris

For the late Michael Graham, a pioneer of ecological planting

Front cover photo:
Veronicastrum virginicum. From a design by Tom Stuart-Smith.
Photo: Catherine Heatherington.

Half-title page photo:
Salvia verticillata 'Purple Rain' and *Stipa gigantea.* From a design by Noël Kingsbury.
Photo: Juliet Sargeant.

Two designs by Oehme and Van Sweden on Long Island, New York (above) and in Indiana (right). The planting closest to the house shows detail and complexity, while sweeps of single herbaceous plants become simpler as they radiate out and merge with the landscape. Photos: John Brookes.

Rosemarie Weisse's prairie garden (right) and steppe garden (below), Westpark, Munich. The plant communities are chosen for their compatibility in vigour and competitiveness, as well as their suitability to the dry, stony habitat. Photos: John Brookes.

Table of Contents

List of Figures and Tabular Information

Plate 1. *Primula elatior* (oxlips), beneath birches at the Jac P. Thijsse Park in The Netherlands.
Photo: Nigel Dunnett

Plate 2. Sculptural yew hedges form a backdrop for the dramatic colour blocks of monarda and helenium at Piet Oudolf's garden in The Netherlands, Summer 2001.
Design: Piet Oudolf
Photo: Catherine Heatherington

1 | INTRODUCTION

Natural, naturalistic and naturalism are frequently used terms, but what is meant by them and what are their inherent qualities? What is naturalism and how do we achieve it?

The *Oxford English Dictionary* describes it as 'a style characterized by a close adherence to nature', but in what way does the designer adhere to nature and when does he or she depart from it? There are many examples of evocative plantings that are clearly artificial, but at the same time able to resonate with the natural environment. The methods used to establish and maintain these plantings are those developed over centuries of horticultural practice, but the natural look is achieved by using combinations that have qualities in common with wild plants. From this point a whole spectrum of naturalistic planting opens up, becoming increasingly like nature in its structural as well as its aesthetic qualities. The schemes at the far end of this range use or mimic the processes of nature in order to achieve the desired effect. It is by establishing complex ecosystems that the designer imbues the planting with a truly naturalistic air.

Naturalism ascribed to designing gardens often encompasses a dynamism that challenges the designer to relinquish or at least loosen control over the years, in order to allow nature to act as a partner in the evolving design. Again, the degree to which the planting is designed to be managed by traditional methods, or allowed to develop naturally, will vary. Plants may or may not be native and the gardening methods can be more or less ecological (see glossary). Nature is abstracted by the designer to a greater or lesser extent, in order to form, not wilderness, but garden that evokes wilderness.

Naturalism is not new at all. People have always vacillated between a wish to impose upon, control and almost eliminate the presence of nature from the garden and an opposing wish to rediscover and enjoy its untamed beauty. Now, with increasing urbanization in the West and the threat of environmental catastrophe world-wide, many are seeking that 'return to nature', not only for the ecological reasons of plant and human survival, but also for the seeming benefits to our sense of well-being, of tuning one's life to natural rhythms and elements. It seems that we no longer want to be alien to our own planet, striving to overcome its forces, but we seek to design with it; we seek 'natural aesthetics'.

This book discusses how a new natural aesthetic has been evolving in Europe and America over the last forty years and examines its different applications. By analysing wild landscapes, elements that conjure up a sense of the natural can be pinpointed and combined with accepted modern design tenets. This establishes useful tools for the garden and landscape designer. In this book there is no foolproof formula for a new perennial planting plan, but a clear foundation for naturalistic work and a broad overview; a pulling together of the strands that will knit to make a new naturalism for the twenty-first century.

The book places the reader within the context of the developing naturalistic garden design movement, giving a sense of its origins and future in the hands of designers working to develop and interpret the genre in their own way.

The starting point is the natural landscape. We 'distil' natural planted sceneries and find the 'essence' of their naturalism. From this we derive 'natural design techniques'. Designers either consciously or instinctively apply these factors to their own plantings. These 'natural techniques' combine well with the accepted modern design tenets such as unity, proportion, rhythm and colour theory to create planting designs that can evoke nature on a smaller scale in the garden.

It is important to discuss the applications of this style of planting and also the practical implications of adopting this method in a maritime climate. Naturalistic planting will

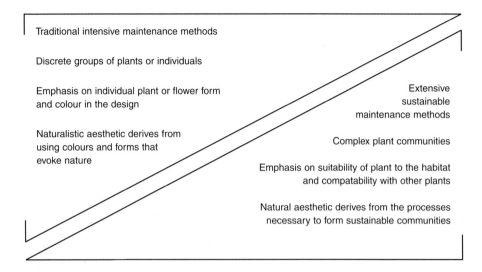

Traditional intensive maintenance methods

Discrete groups of plants or individuals

Emphasis on individual plant or flower form and colour in the design

Naturalistic aesthetic derives from using colours and forms that evoke nature

Extensive sustainable maintenance methods

Complex plant communities

Emphasis on suitability of plant to the habitat and compatability with other plants

Natural aesthetic derives from the processes necessary to form sustainable communities

Fig. 1.1 Gradient summary

The term naturalistic can be applied to a variety of horticultural methods and design applications. This is illustrated as a gradient from intensive methods and a traditional design strategy to extensive maintenance methods and the design effects that derive from them.

undoubtedly relate well to natural landscapes, but can it be applied as easily to other environments? What is the relationship between naturalistic gardens and architecture? Does one dictate the other? Scale, is an important issue, as is the relationship between planting and the overall design of the garden. Will it only succeed within an informal framework, or does it require containment within a formal structure?

Questions relating to design or planting style are best addressed in relation to specific plant combinations and existing gardens. For this reason we have included chapters to look at examples of naturalistic plantings, with drawings and plans for clarity.

We are indebted to several designers working in this field today, who have generously contributed their thoughts and ideas to the debate. Many of them gave us practical insights, which we have included throughout the book.

The chapter on preparation and general maintenance will help the designer to address the question of whether this style of planting is suitable for a particular scheme, or which adaptation would best suit. Some of the adaptations are high maintenance with intensive methods of cultivation. Others are very low maintenance. It is essential for the success and development of a scheme that both designer and client are aware of its future requirements.

This has always been the case with designed areas of planting. The difference now, with naturalistic planting, is that designer and client can see natural forces of change within the plant communities as a positive contribution to the scheme. This may well involve the designer in an element of explanation and education. This book will clarify the theory behind the naturalistic planting movement and enable the individual to develop practical working processes.

2 RECENT DEVELOPMENTS IN NATURALISTIC PLANTING

A dualism between art and culture on the one side and nature on the other has long run through the history of Western garden design. Gardens, be they wild and natural or formal and ordered, are examples of human control over nature. Classical designs seek to create harmonious order within the landscape, whilst romanticism aims to perfect the powerful wilderness.

Considered by many to be the forerunner of the naturalistic movement, William Robinson (1838-1935), developed an understanding of how plants grow in the wild and advocated the grouping of plants with similar needs, which were then encouraged to naturalize. His work can be seen as a reaction to the Industrial Revolution with its increasing urbanization and newfound power over natural resources. He sought to turn the viewer's eye back to the subtleties of natural forms and colours.

Gertrude Jekyll (1843-1932), worked within the formal Edwardian design layout, but championed the use of perennials and their combination into less formal and more naturalistic planting designs. However, people were still kept at a distance from the plants, which were often planted in serried ranks and graduated colours. Viewing the plants was inevitably a two-dimensional experience with the viewer being kept to the front of the long herbaceous border.

In Northern Europe designers and nurserymen examined the habitats and groupings of plants in the wild – their form and structure as well as their distribution and companion plantings. In Germany Karl Foerster (1874-1970), a nurseryman and plant breeder, brought a new palette of grasses, tall perennials and non-hybridized plants to the attention of the designer.

While Foerster was collecting and developing new plants, Jac P. Thijsse (1865-1944) in The Netherlands was focusing on the education of the public, especially children, into an appreciation of natural systems.

His park, Thijsse's Hof, opened in 1926, was the first 'Heem Park'. These Dutch ecological parks are created in urban neighbourhoods with the intention of bringing nature to the towns and suburbs. Heem Parks spread throughout The Netherlands, making creative use of the natural surroundings and habitats by the careful selection of solely native species (Plate 1). Maintenance can be high, but the process is a dynamic one – the patterns of plantings developing and changing in time and space. Ironically habitats become more fertile with the build-up of leaf litter and organic matter and hence require higher maintenance over time.

With the advent of the Modernist Movement in the 1920s and '30s, gardeners began to move away from not only the formality of the Edwardian era but, more importantly for planting, the symmetry. Japanese design brought a new way of relating to plants and a greater understanding of their relationship with the space around them, encouraging the viewer to experience the garden from different positions.

In parallel with this renewed understanding of plants and the increasing influence of the conservationists came an emphasis on low-maintenance planting. This was initially a pragmatic response to client requirements, but has now developed into a driving force behind the argument for the use of native and naturalistic planting. Clients often require low maintenance gardens and also desire to 'get back to nature'.

The conservationists' interest in a plant's natural habitat was taken up by Richard Hansen and Friedrich Stahl with their book *Perennials and their Garden Habitats*,[1] first published in Germany in 1981 and later in Britain in 1993. They defined two types of perennials.[2] First is

---

[1] Hansen, R. and Stahl, F. *Perennials and Their Garden Habitats*. Cambridge University Press, 1993.
[2] Ward, R. 'Harmony in Wild Planting'. *Landscape Design*, December 89/January 90.

the border perennial, an exotic, hybridized and therefore demanding plant requiring high maintenance and, importantly, no competition. Border perennials need plenty of space around the individual plants; hence weeding, dividing and replanting become the job of the gardener. Second, wild perennials by contrast are less hybridized and more able to withstand the pressures of competing individuals. Hansen and Stahl were not advocating a 'natives-only' approach to planting; rather their book sought to give practical advice about plant combinations for differing garden habitats based on their ecological characteristics.

Many German designers were inspired by the work of Hansen and Stahl and, in 1983, Rosemarie Weisse created a garden in Munich Westpark (see p.v), which she describes as an exaggeration of nature. The site is a 2200m^2 gravel pit, with poor, infertile soil and good drainage. Weisse created winding paths through loose sweeps of intricately woven perennials.[3] The plant communities are not necessarily native and do not always occur together in the wild. They are chosen, however, for their compatibility in vigour and competitiveness as well as their suitability to the dry, stony habitat. A benefit of the extremes

of climate is that in winter the dead or dying plant material is under snow for several months.[4]

The design of this scheme, and others which followed in Germany, has very little structural framework and few borders or boundaries.[5] To appreciate it the visitor has to walk amongst the plantings, to get up close. Often such designs are created with no reference to the built environment.

In parallel with the more naturalistic planting schemes developing in Germany, two designers based in the US captured the public's imagination with their interpretation of the European model for the American landscape. Wolfgang Oehme and James van Sweden changed the face of American gardening, advocating the uprooting of the lawn and the planting of perennials. The resulting designs are stylized prairies with great sweeps of grasses and tall herbaceous plants. In contrast with many European designers, Oehme and van Sweden work with large masses of one variety of plant or huge blocks of grasses to create transitions and boundaries.

Oehme and van Sweden's designs are often for large private gardens, where the link between plants and the house is as important as with the landscape beyond the garden. Closest to the house is detail and complexity, the planting becoming simpler as it radiates out and finally merges with the landscape (see p.vi). As at Westpark, when standing in the midst of the

planting masses, the visitor can appreciate the design from all sides.

French interpretations of the naturalistic planting movement have evolved from the early models. Gilles Clément is acclaimed for his Jardin en Mouvement at the Parc André Citroën. The Jardin is one element within the formal structure of the Parisian park.[6] Grasses and wildflowers were sown without any exact idea of how they would develop over time. The Jardin constantly changes, the designer defining parameters, and the plants and visitors taking over. Mowing creates pathways, but they too can change over time. The movement of the garden's title thus relates to both the movement of flowers and grasses in the wind and through the seasons, and also to the dynamism allowed into the process.

In The Netherlands Piet Oudolf has embedded naturalistic planting in the public consciousness. His schemes use large blocks of colour and form repeated through space. They work best on a large scale, often remote from buildings, but in smaller gardens structure is incorporated by clipping box, yew and ornamental pear to form walls and buttresses (Plate 2). Like many other naturalistic plantings it is important for the viewer to get amongst the plants and experience the design on different levels – from a tapestry of colour, through a contrast of

[3] Kingsbury, N. and von Schoenaich, B. 'Learning from Nature'. *The Garden*, June 1995.
[4] Van Groeningen, I. 'Natural Choices'. *The Garden*, October, 1995.
[5] Lacey, S. 'Steppe into the Garden'. *The Garden Design Journal*, Volume 2, Issue 2, Summer, 1995.

[6] Trulove, J. *Designed Landscape Forum*. Spacemaker Press, Washington DC, 1998.

forms, to the detail of individual flower-heads and leaf-shapes.

For some designers naturalistic planting demands informality of design and a dynamism that echoes natural forces. The use of gravel pioneered by Mrs Robinson, and subsequently John Brookes, at Denmans in the 1970s, allows for flowing lines and indistinct boundaries between plants and people. Plants self-seed into paths which wander casually through the plants (Plate 3). Indeed paths may even change direction as dictated by the plants.

Beth Chatto also experimented with this version of naturalistic planting. Like Hansen, her starting point was to explore how the plants developed in their natural habitat. Her dry gravel garden is reminiscent of Weisse's Munich Westpark: winding gravel paths, dry conditions and plants which are allowed to seed themselves within the confines of the informal beds (Plate 4).

The design of informal beds and winding paths are referred to by Noël Kingsbury as 'open borders'.[7] The plant types are native or naturalistic and the physical relationship of the viewer to the plants is intimate, thus reflecting a contemporary desire to 'get close to' or 'return to' nature.

There is much debate about the application of the European or the US naturalistic models to

---

[7] Kingsbury, N. *The New Perennial Garden*. Frances Lincoln, London, 1996.

CULTURE   NATURE

Desire for low maintenance
Awareness of heritage – traditional processes and landscapes
Desire for connection with the 'wild'
Use of materials – gravel
Media influences
Education
Plant breeding

A Naturalistic Planting Ethos

Environmental awareness
Interest in conservation
Interest in plant habitats
Trial gardens – reclamation of contaminated land
Wildlife gardens
Native plants
Compatible plant groupings

Reaction to formality

Impressionistic colour schemes

Modernism — the Japanese influence

Asymmetry

Abstract expressionism

ART

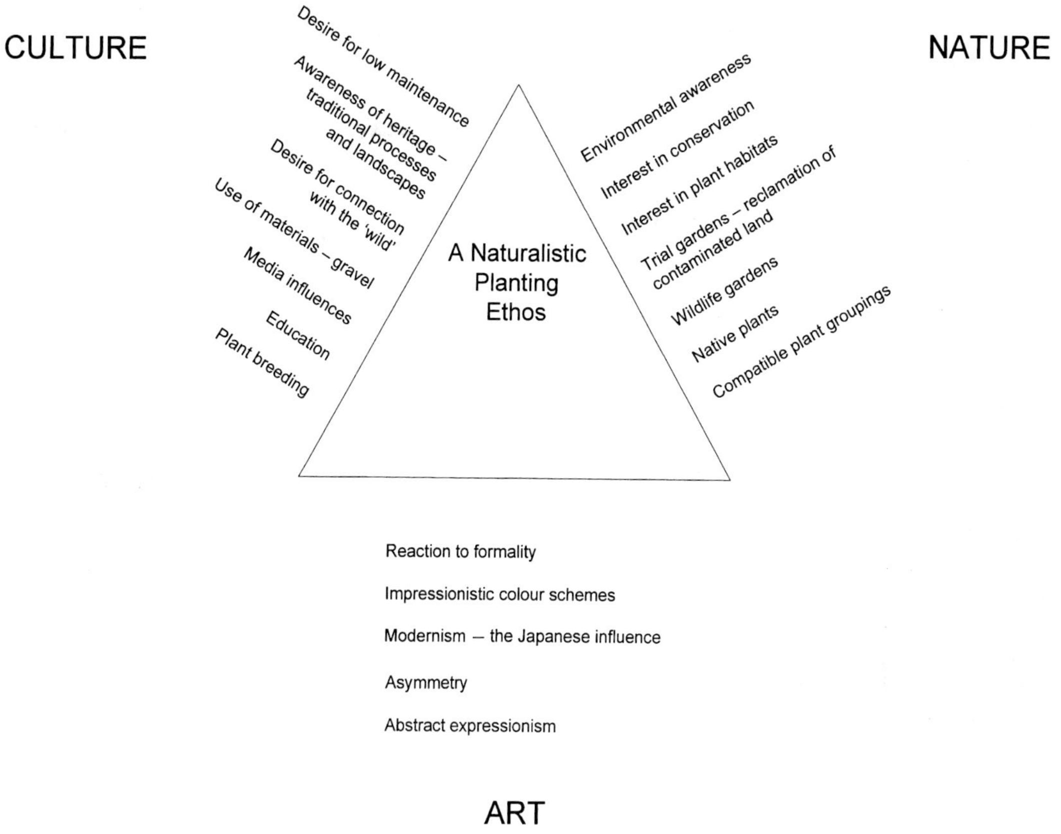

Fig. 2.1 The development of a naturalistic ethos

warmer, maritime climates, without the snow cover to hide unsightly bare earth during the winter. A wet autumn and winter can leave dead flower and seed heads a soggy mass and often the early spring climate is mild, encouraging weed growth and slug grazing on the new perennial shoots. This calls for a naturalistic design framework, which can work within such specific ecological and climatic conditions.

NOËL KINGSBURY

Noël Kingsbury gained a deep understanding of plants from practical experience running his own nursery. His design skills are mostly self-taught, which has served to free him from many of the constraints of traditional dogma. Although initially influenced by twentieth-century English gardening and design tradition, he has become increasingly interested in the work of designers who are inspired by nature and who seek to work ecologically. His most formative reading has been the work of Richard Hansen, and in 1994 a visit to the Munich Westpark completely changed his design ethos and the direction of his work.

I am self-taught, so I have avoided being driven down paths of inevitability. Much of what I have learned has been through talking to practitioners and seeing what they have done.

Planting Philosophy

Kingsbury approaches design from a plant-centred direction, and his first inspiration is nature. Having worked at first with wild flowers and ecological plantings, he now applies that body of knowledge to creating ecological plantings with non-native species. Seasonal interest and colour are less important than the suitability of the plants to the site and to each other.

Kingsbury's approach to gardening and maintenance is as near to sustainable as practically possible, but he is not uncompromisingly 'organic', believing that there is a small, but crucial role for herbicides in soil preparation and weed control.

Part of the excitement of this new area are the benefits that accrue from the need to look across traditional professional boundaries. It is only by doing this that we can fully realize the potential of our garden plant heritage.

I do not believe in using fertilizers and soil modification. Essential to this philosophy is the belief that, however awful the soil, nature has a beautiful flora to choose from that will thrive.

Advice

- Look at plants in decorative natural habitats, such as cliff-top meadows and Mediterranean maquis. Try to get a feel for how the plants grow together and how they are distributed across space. Botanic gardens can be a good source of inspiration, because they are increasingly being arranged biogeographically to reproduce natural communities.
- Study plant ecology.
- Take the opportunity to visit gardens in Holland and Germany first-hand.
- Get to know plants that are appropriate for the ecology of the places in which you will be working. Grow them yourself if you really want to understand their life-cycles intimately. Plant knowledge is potentially never ending and it takes a long time to accumulate.
- Be prepared to experiment and closely monitor the results.

Planting Combinations
(see Plates 6, 7, 8)

Spring and early summer:
- *Geranium x oxonianum* cvs,
- Blue geraniums, e.g. *Geranium* 'Johnson's Blue',
- *Calamagrostis x acutiflora* 'Karl Foerster',
- *Aster* 'Climax',
- *Persicaria bistorta* 'Superba',
- *Euphorbia palustris*.

Autumn:
- *Aster* 'Little Carlow',
- *Aster turbinellus*,
- *Solidago rugosa* 'Fireworks',
- *Helianthus* 'Lemon Queen',
- *Miscanthus sinensis*,
- *Rudbeckia fulgida*,
- *Carex comans*,
- *Stipa arundinacea*.

Gardens Open to the Public:
Cowley Manor.
Webbs of Wychbold.

Contact Details:
www.landsol.com

3 SUSTAINABILITY AND PLANTING DESIGN

Throughout the twentieth century the work of ecologists and conservationists has influenced the naturalistic planting movement. At one extreme the use of solely native plants is advocated as the only way to achieve a 'natural' scheme. A less dogmatic approach is to consider in detail the suitability of the site and its varied habitats when selecting plants, and to allow the introduction of exotics to create a desired effect and increase biodiversity.

A sustainable environment[1] is one that both meets the needs of the present generation and does not compromise adversely those of future generations. Sustainability is concerned with resource management. The energy, fertilizers, pesticides and water required to build and maintain a landscape are minimized, and the biodiversity and productivity of the site are kept as close as possible to the natural level or increased. Thus, in terms of planting design, a bedding scheme, with its high levels of maintenance and waste, is unsustainable – as is weeding, staking, dividing and feeding a traditional herbaceous border (Fig 3.1).

A totally sustainable model is appealing ideologically, but human activity must also

---

[1] Dunnett, N. and Hitchmough, J. 'Excitement and Energy'. *Landscape Design*, June 1996.

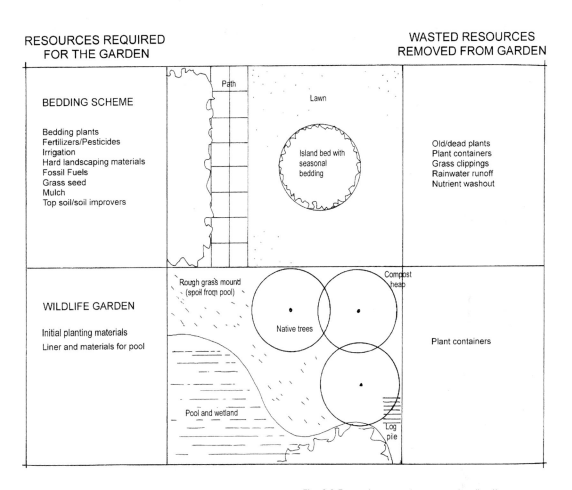

RESOURCES REQUIRED FOR THE GARDEN

WASTED RESOURCES REMOVED FROM GARDEN

BEDDING SCHEME

Bedding plants
Fertilizers/Pesticides
Irrigation
Hard landscaping materials
Fossil Fuels
Grass seed
Mulch
Top soil/soil improvers

Path

Lawn

Island bed with seasonal bedding

Old/dead plants
Plant containers
Grass clippings
Rainwater runoff
Nutrient washout

WILDLIFE GARDEN

Initial planting materials
Liner and materials for pool

Rough grass mound (spoil from pool)

Compost heap

Native trees

Plant containers

Pool and wetland

Log pile

Fig. 3.1 Ecosystems and resource implications

form a part of the ecological equation. If a planting scheme is unattractive or the level of informality unacceptable, especially in an urban situation, the planting will fail through lack of interest.

The public perception of ecological design is often a 'natives only' approach. Yet many countries have a long history of plant collecting, and maritime climates are able to sustain many new species and varieties. Native species have the advantage over imports in that they are already adapted to the site and therefore require fewer resources. However, in the warm microclimates of our cities exotics are often better suited, add interest and excitement, and can also increase wildlife diversity by extending the flowering season. Many sustainable planting schemes use a combination of natives and exotics with the proviso that exotics should never be used in situations where they may naturalize into the surrounding countryside.

Site Characteristics

The natural habitat of the plants is more important than the country of origin. A 'steppe' planting on dry, well-drained and infertile soil may combine *Stipa gigantea*, a native of Spain and Portugal, with *Iris attica* from north-west Turkey and *Euphorbia myrsinites* from southern Europe and North Africa, and the result will be both sustainable and aesthetically pleasing.

A detailed analysis of the site is required before creating a sustainable planting scheme. Rather than choosing plants and then creating a habitat to fit their requirements, as in traditional horticultural practice, the habitat is analysed and the appropriate plants selected. Even a small garden has a variety of microclimates, from shade beneath a tree to a sunny, well-drained raised bed next to the house. The following factors should be considered when determining the types of planting schemes possible:

Soil
• What are the properties of the soil?
• What is the pH value?

Aspect
• Where is the sun?
• Which areas of the garden are in full sun and which in shade?

Drainage
• Is it a well-drained sandy soil or a water-logged heavy clay?
• Are there areas of the garden which are always wet?

Climate/Microclimate
• Does the garden have frost pockets or sheltered areas?
• Is the site windy or sheltered?
• Are there any other unusual climatic conditions?

Fertility
• Is the soil fertility high or low?

Existing vegetation
• Are there existing plants which can be incorporated in the design?
• Can this help when choosing new plant communities for the site?
• What plants are growing in the surrounding area?

Plant Characteristics

If a community is to be sustainable, plants must be chosen with regard to their competitiveness:[2] a vigorous species can easily swamp a slower-growing neighbour. Broadly speaking plants fall into three categories:[3]

1. Competitors are vigorous and large-growing, especially on fertile soil or with the addition of nutrients, for example, *Anemone x hybrida*.
2. Stress tolerators are slower-growing and do not respond to the addition of nutrients as strongly as competitors. They naturally occur in habitats where resources are limited, for example, *Helleborus orientalis*, tolerant of drought and low light-levels.
3. Ruderals grow vigorously to take advantage of transient conditions, but are short-lived, reproducing successfully by seed, for example, *Aquilegia vulgaris*.

Useful plants for ecological schemes often possess a combination of characteristics: for

---

[2] Hitchmough, J. 'Natural Neighbours'. *Landscape Design*, April 1994.
[3] Grime, J. P. *Plant Strategies and Vegetation Processes*. 2nd ed. John Wiley, Chichester, 2002.

Plate 4. *Allium sphaerocephalon* creates random spots of intense colour as *Stipa tenuissima* and *Eryngium giganteum* seed through a gravel garden in Essex which is never watered.
Design: Beth Chatto
Photo: Juliet Sargeant

Plate 5. *Eryngium giganteum* self-seeds through the graveyard at Bolton Percy, Yorkshire, Autumn 2001.
Design: Roger Brook
Photo: Catherine Heatherington

Plate 3. *Sisyrinchium striatum, Digitalis purpurea* and *Verbascum olympicum* sow themselves naturally into gravel at Denmans Garden, West Sussex, June 2000.
Design: John Brookes
Photo: Juliet Sargeant

Plate 6. *Persicaria amplexicaulis* and *Lythrum salicaria.*
Design: Noël Kingsbury
Photo: Juliet Sargeant

Plate 7. The flowerheads of *Helianthus* 'Lemon Queen' share space with those of *Miscanthus sinensis* in Noël Kingsbury's garden on the Welsh border.
Design: Noël Kingsbury
Photo: Juliet Sargeant

Plate 8. Intermingling naturalistic planting at Cowley Manor, Gloucestershire, August 1997.
Design: Noël Kingsbury
Photo: Juliet Sargeant

Plate 10. *Campanula lactiflora* and *Achillea grandifolia* form part of a successional planting scheme in a tiny front garden. Spring flowers in the scheme include geranium, aquilegia and primrose, July 2002.
Design: Nigel Dunnett
Photo: Catherine Heatherington

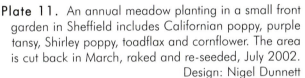

Plate 11. An annual meadow planting in a small front garden in Sheffield includes Californian poppy, purple tansy, Shirley poppy, toadflax and cornflower. The area is cut back in March, raked and re-seeded, July 2002.
Design: Nigel Dunnett
Seed mix from Pictorial Meadows
Photo: Catherine Heatherington

Plate 9. This experimental roof garden in Sheffield demonstrates the use of a wide range of intermingling perennial plants and grasses including species of kniphofia, perennial wallflower and festuca, July 2002.
Design: Nigel Dunnett
Photo: Catherine Heatherington

Plate 12. *Helleborus foetidus* gives winter interest to this small-scale successional planting scheme which includes late flowering *Geranium psilostemon* and *Campanula lactiflora*, July 2002.
Design: Nigel Dunnett
Photo: Catherine Heatherington

Plate 15. The complex intermingling of different leaf and flower forms in a wild hedgerow habitat in southern England.
Photo: Juliet Sargeant

Plate 13. Sunlight filters through the tree canopy of an English bluebell wood. Vertical stems arise from the dramatic blue of the ground plane.
Photo: Juliet Sargeant

Plate 14. The natural dispersion of moisture-loving plants is illustrated in this Scottish wetland.
Photo: Catherine Heatherington

Plate 16. Marram grass forms drifts through the sand.
Photo: Juliet Sargeant

example, stress-tolerant competitors such as geraniums and the stress-tolerant ruderal, *Digitalis purpurea*, both survive in drought conditions. Nutrient-stress leads to slower growth and longer life.[4] Many naturalistic planting schemes require low fertility, which encourages less vigorous growth and therefore reduces the need to stake plants, and also enables stress-tolerant flowering species to compete successfully with the more nutrient-needy grasses in a flowering meadow.

Design Considerations[5]

Restoring humans to the ecological equation requires a level of understanding from both the designer and the general public. The aesthetic qualities of the design must not be lost with the desire for an ecological framework. The context of the design may determine the planting; in a wildlife or urban regeneration scheme, a native-only approach may be the answer, but alternative solutions are needed when combining planting with architecture in an urban setting.

The basic tenets of design, such as structure, unity and the manipulation of space, apply equally to sustainable and more traditional designs. Planting schemes work in three dimensions and ecological design creates tiers of vegetation; plants occupy different spaces in different seasons. Lower-growing bulbs or perennials create mats close to the ground in the spring, giving way to more vigorous neighbours as summer progresses. The succession of plants brings structure and increases the diversity of textures and forms throughout the year.

Unity in design is most effectively achieved by restricting the palette, both in the variety of plants and their colour. This, however is a compromise which will reduce biodiversity. Alternatively a matrix of plants (see glossary) can be built up to create a repeating mass of vegetation. In some cases grasses form the basis of the matrix, as in a meadow. In others they may be only one element within the more complex matrix of self-regulating perennials.

Sustainable planting also brings fundamental new design considerations. The loosening of traditional methods of control introduces an element of dynamism to the design. Individual plants change with the season, as does the relationship between plants within the group. Self-seeding brings excitement and movement to the composition. Such designs also encourage the examination of intricacy and the appreciation of detail. It is essential that the viewer be invited into the planting to experience it on multiple levels.

Naturalistic planting can range from the sustainable to the purely aesthetic. Later chapters look at various naturalistic designs and the balance they achieve between the two extremes. Here two sustainable planting schemes are discussed. Both are examples of biotope planting: a community resembling a natural habitat but with a mix of species chosen for both aesthetic and ecological reasons.[6]

Bolton Percy

The churchyard at Bolton Percy in Yorkshire, planted and managed by Roger Brook for 25 years,[7] is a mass of dynamic planting both native and exotic. The garden has been allowed to evolve over the years with minimal intervention, and the gravestones are surrounded by drifts of ground cover such as *Euphorbia amygdaloides* var. *robbiae, Galium odoratum, Geranium macrorrhizum, Sedum spectabile* and *Lamium galeobdolon* through which taller flowering perennials emerge during the summer months. *Stipa arundinacea* and *Eryngium giganteum* self-seed as do aquilegias, honesty, poppies and forget-me-nots (Plate 5). Weeds are kept under control by hand-pulling or hoeing but not by digging. Any deep-rooted weeds are killed with a spot application of glyphosate, and the dead plant allowed to

---

[4] For a discussion of plant longevity see Hitchmough, J. 'Natural Neighbours'. *Landscape Design*, April 1994.
[5] Dunnett, N. 'Harnessing Anarchy'. *Landscape Design*, November 1995.

[6] Dunnett, N. and Hitchmough J., Eds, *The Dynamic Landscape: Design and Ecology of Landscape Vegetation.* Spon Press, 2004.
[7] Dunnett, N. 'Tending God's Acre'. *The Garden*, December 2000.

decompose *in situ*. This absence of digging avoids soil disturbance and hence discourages the germination of weed seeds.

Small-scale Successional Planting

Nigel Dunnett at Sheffield University has conducted trials in the field of sustainable planting in Britain, and his own garden demonstrates successional and ecological planting on a small scale (Plate 12). Dunnett's understanding of how the plant combinations develop through the seasons ensures that his plantings have year-round interest – essential in a small space. A conventional plan is of no use with such a scheme and Dunnett looks at the proportions of each type of plant dependent on their flowering season (Fig. 3.2). He uses smaller numbers of early-flowering perennials, often woodland-edge plants which will emerge to give a carpet of green in the spring, but will be happy in semi-shade later in the year. These are followed by a larger proportion of the taller-growing perennials which keep their form and seedheads into the autumn and winter. Simple examples are primroses beneath campanulas and geraniums or astilbes in a carpet of wood anemones (Fig. 3.3).

Evergreen/winter interest
N = native
Helleborus foetidus N
Matteuccia struthiopteris
Calamagrostis x acutiflora 'Karl Foerster'
Early flowering
Geranium sylvaticum N
Aquilegia vulgaris N
Primula vulgaris N
Late flowering
Campanula lactiflora
Geranium psilostemon
Achillea grandiflora
Lythrum salicaria N
Helianthus 'Lemon Queen'

Fig. 3.3 Small-scale successional planting scheme

Planting for succession	Percentage of mix
Structural grasses	20%
Spring flowering perennials	20%
Summer flowering perennials	30%
Autumn flowering perennials	30%
Bulbs	scattered at high density

Fig. 3.2 Percentages for successional planting

- Observe how the plant grows in its natural habitat.
- Match plant communities to the site conditions.
- Avoid disturbance to the soil after planting.
- Exotics can add to diversity.
- Be cautious when using exotics in situations where they may naturalize or become invasive.
- Consider the limited use of glyphosate for the eradication of perennial weeds.

PRACTITIONER PROFILE

NIGEL DUNNETT

Nigel Dunnett undertakes research into the application of ecological concepts to landscape and garden planting.

I developed my ideas independently while still quite young and then discovered that there were many other people thinking the same way. I have been very much affected by the Dutch 'Heem Parks' and nature gardens.

Dunnett has worked on a range of experimental large and small-scale public planting schemes in and around Sheffield. A few of the many examples of his work include: roof gardens planted with a combination of low-growing perennials and grasses; perennial planting in urban regeneration schemes; the creation of a commercially available annual meadow seed mix; and experiments with coppiced woodland and perennial ground cover.

Because I spent a lot of time when I was growing up plant hunting in natural habitats, I gradually came to realize that the sense of exhilaration and 'perfection' that I found when observing plants in the wild was not being matched by the feelings I felt in gardens. I therefore decided to see if I could reproduce some of these effects.

Planting Philosophy

I'm really not interested in the individual plant, but more in how they work en masse.

In his plantings Dunnett aims to combine sustainability with aesthetics to create successional planting schemes. He rarely works with detailed planting plans but instead develops randomly planted or sown, ecologically and aesthetically-compatible mixtures (Plates 9, 10, 11, 12). He starts with four basic design tools:

- Colour balance;
- Phenology – the growth habits and flowering pattern of a plant over the year – informs the choice of plants giving year-round interest and a naturalistic intermingling of plant forms through three dimensions;
- Structural diversity – achieving an aesthet-ically pleasing balance of forms and heights;
- Ecological compatibility – ensuring plant choices match each other in terms of competitive ability and are also suited to the site.

In addition, locality, a knowledge of the local landscape, the plants that grow there and how they grow is very important; as is an understanding of the traditional processes involved in creating landscape.

Advice

- Forget planting plans. Instead develop a mixture-based approach to using perennials and grasses by creating planting specifications that can be placed almost randomly, in much the same way as a naturalistic woodland may be established. The skill comes in plant selection and the various proportions of the different species, rather than very detailed placing of individual plant next to individual plant as in more traditional planting design.
- Complete perennial weed control is essential. High planting density at the outset helps.
- Local character and distinctiveness is important – abstracting elements from regional vegetation types and patterns.
- Aesthetics are paramount – if it does not look good and colourful then it is unlikely to be maintained and therefore may be unsustainable in the long term.
- Emphasize the contrast between geometry and naturalistic forms when designing for the urban environment or for smaller-scale projects.

Planting Combinations

Dunnett works with seed mixes and randomly planted mixtures, so the concept of plant associations is less relevant (Plate 11).

Seed mixes are available from Pictorial Meadows.
Web: www.pictorialmeadows.co.uk

Planting Schemes open to the Public

Fairleigh Gateway.
Sheffield General Cemetery.
Woodland Garden, Sheffield Botanical Gardens.

Contact Details:

Dr Nigel Dunnett, Department of Landscape, University of Sheffield, Arts Tower, Western Bank, Sheffield S10 2TN.
Tel: 0114 222 0611. Fax: 0114 275 4176
www.shef.ac.uk/landscape/research.html

4 NATURAL DESIGN TECHNIQUES

The self-regulating plant communities described in Chapter 3 are dependent on a weaving of different species into a sustainable matrix. This intermingling closely approaches the way plants behave in their natural habitats. However, many patterns in spontaneous natural planting lend themselves to a more abstracted interpretation in design terms, and it is often these that the designer draws on for inspiration. For example, a bluebell wood evokes feelings of nostalgia, peace and perhaps drama by repetition, colour and the play of light and shadow. The picture from the roadside or footpath is of a carpet of blue, enticing the visitor into the wood to experience the intricacies of the flowers themselves and the change in the quality of the light.

A visual analysis reveals a plane of dramatic ground-colour punctuated by the vertical accents of deciduous trees. Shafts of light pull the eye to the horizontal plane of incandescent blue, and the visitor is drawn into the woodland, where the eye travels up the vertical tree trunks, completing the three-dimensional space (Plate 13).

Similar analysis of other natural scenes leads to the creation of a naturalistic design palette to be used alongside the fundamental planting design tenets of form, texture, colour and repetition.

Intermingling

Intermingling is a close approximation to nature; small communities of plants intermingle with larger groups and individuals, their flower heads sharing the same space (Plate 15). Hedgerows and verges are a mass of plants in a jumble of colour, form and distribution, although the competition between plant communities may lead to a few species dominating. This dynamic planting is often in flux with some species taking over, and then losing their advantage when environmental conditions change.

To the viewer this mix of many colours and forms is likely to be less restful than larger drifts and sweeps with a more limited plant palette.

Natural Dispersion

Seed dispersal ensures that a new plant will germinate some distance from the parent so it does not have to compete for space and food. A patch of bare earth is an invitation for seeds, and animals play a part in the reproductive cycle by rooting up plants, leaving open space for the next generation.

Visually large clumps give way to smaller groupings and then to individual plants, some distance from the parent. The eye of the viewer settles first on the larger groups, and then is taken on a radiating path which becomes ever more random (Fig. 4.1).

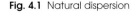

Fig. 4.1 Natural dispersion

Natural dispersion is recognizable in many plant communities, including foxgloves in light woodland, naturalized bulbs in meadows and cowslips in rough grass. The matrix ground cover in these cases is predominantly green, usually grass, but dispersion is not restricted to meadowland and occurs naturally in leafmould, gravel or shingle and wetlands (Plate 14).

Drifts

A further expression of the natural dispersion of plants is the formation of large sweeps or drifts. This occurs rarely in nature, but it can be seen in the drifting of a single species through shingle or stony ground: for example, *Crambe cordifolia* above the tideline, *Eschscholzia californica* (Californian poppies) along dry, rocky verges or *Ammophila arenaria* (marram grass) in sand (Plate 16). A drift becomes recognizable within a complex plant community when one species is more visually dominant than its neighbours.

In design terms the simplicity of drifts is appealing and two or three plants can be combined in large sweeps with a blurring of their boundaries (Fig. 4.2). These groupings vary with one colour or shape taking precedence over the others at different times or seasons. The movement and repetition between the drifts creates a fluidity which leads the eye around the landscape. Often such sweeps are best appreciated on a grand scale.

Fig. 4.2 Drifts

Random Scattering

Verges and meadows are a random and dynamic mix of herbaceous plants and grasses competing and coexisting with their neighbours. Individual success or failure will vary from one year to the next. The visual effect is of random spots of colour on a green background in a primarily two-dimensional plane (Plate 17).

This type of planting is characterized by small areas of colour, and from a distance there is little visible form. It is often the setting of the meadow that completes the overall picture, by creating a background and enclosing the horizontal plane within a structure of 'walls' such as a mountain range or woodland edge.

Within the meadow itself there is rarely a focal point and there is no middle ground. Getting up close and in amongst the planting brings the subtle variety of forms into focus and creates the foreground, which is lacking from a distance. The eye moves randomly and quickly from one point to another without settling; colour becomes the essential element. The combination of colours that occurs in nature, although seemingly harmonious, would often be thought to clash in another setting, and it is the background of green that mutes the intensity and jarring.

Key/Accent Plants

Natural focal points occur when striking vertical elements grow within a horizontal understorey

Fig. 4.3 Accents

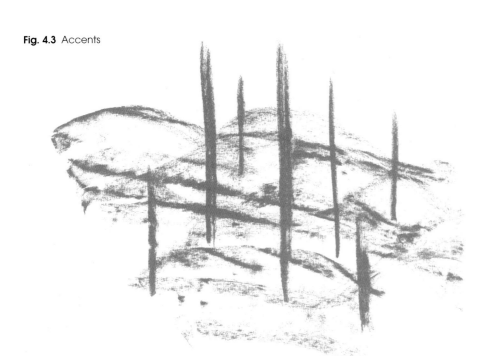

trees punctuating a scrubby ground cover form an imposing three-dimensional composition through the year. Change is evident in the quality of light penetrating the canopy and the resulting growth beneath.

Planes

Large expanses of reeds stretching to the horizon, or tapestries of heather on hillsides, can be abstracted by the designer into a combination of horizontal and vertical planes (Fig. 4.4). The sheer scale of these plantings brings its own drama and the movement both of wind and light create a dynamic force which engages the eye. The horizontal plane is usually juxtaposed with the vertical backdrop of sky, hills or trees completing the three-dimensional picture (Plate 19).

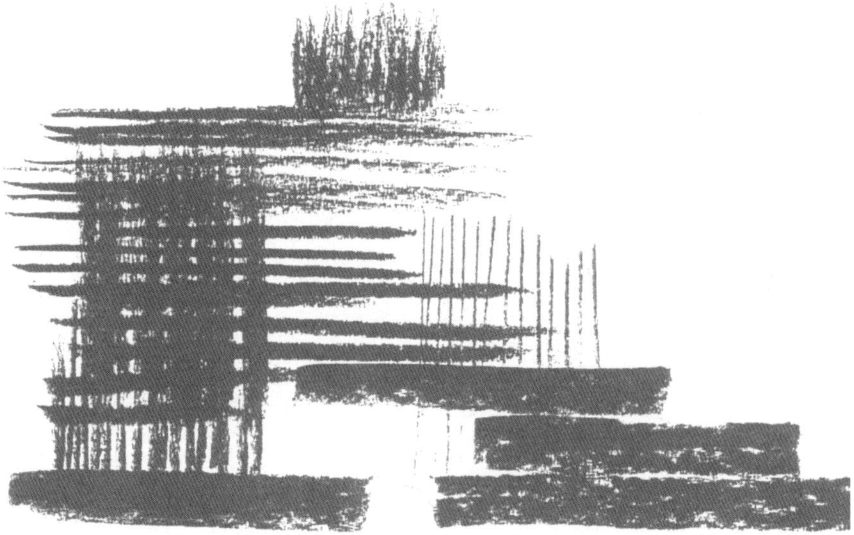

(Fig. 4.3). The eye scans horizontally and rests on the vertical, moving from one dramatic form to another. Examples are ferns in a woodland ground cover of native anemones or teazels in a field (Plate 18).

Perennial accent plants give an element of drama or surprise to a scene which may appear static for much of the year. For example, the random colour wash of a meadow often takes on a three-dimensional element as summer progresses.

By contrast the permanent accents created by

Fig. 4.4 Planes

Fig. 4.5 Blocks

The seven design techniques described in this chapter are a result of an analysis and abstraction of natural plant communities. They are chosen for their ability to be replicated within the defined space of a garden. For the designer they must be refined and combined with the basic tenets of unity, simplicity, balance, scale and proportion. As happens in nature, the designer will often choose more than one technique to achieve the desired naturalism. These are the tools and it is by disregarding formulae and applying the principles creatively that an atmospheric space evoking nature can be achieved.

KEY POINTS

- The distant view, the middle ground and the detail are all significant in the natural landscape.
- Nature does not always respect colour theory.
- The grand scale in the natural landscape cannot always be used in design, so other features must be incorporated for visual impact.
- The process of natural dispersion gives unity and rhythm to a planting, which creates cohesion and a sense of familiarity.

It is worth considering in this context the agrarian landscape which forms a large section of familiar countryside in many areas. The rectilinear plantings of planes of wheat, oilseed rape or vegetables divided by lines of green hedges, verge or set-aside meadow planting can in no way be considered natural. However, the technique of layering planes within a landscape can be extrapolated to a more naturalistic design.

Blocks

The sustainable plant communities formed by perennials compatible in vigour, competitiveness and life expectancy may be characterized visually in terms of either colour or form. For example, the garish patches of yellow and green lichen creeping over limestone rocks can appear as distinct blocks (Fig. 4.5). This is unusual, however; in most natural landscapes the visual simplicity of the repeating blocks of colour belies a complex intermingling process (Plate 20).

The designer simplifies such plantings into repeating blocks of colour or form, creating a rhythm which pulls the visitor into and around the space. Once amongst the planting the detail of form, scent and texture holds the attention.

5 NATURALISTIC MATRICES

The word matrix can be used to describe the layers of vegetation which make up an intermingling or random-scattering planting scheme.[1] The roots below the surface, the mat-forming plants, happy in the semi-shade, and the layer of taller sun-loving perennials, coexist in a sustainable plant community. Designs using matrices imitate nature closely and do not lend themselves to conventional planting plans, based as they are on random mixes of species rather than larger groups of one plant.

The four planting schemes discussed in this chapter all use the intermingling model as their starting point. In some cases individual plants are placed completely randomly on a grid or based on a density per square metre. In others the designer considers the effect of placing two plants together or of judiciously grouping plants to give the impression of their having dispersed naturally.

Intermingling with Accents

Noël Kingsbury has planted a display area for Webbs of Wychbold in Worcestershire, which uses a system of 'sample' planting plans (Figs. 5.1 & 5.2). Each sample is carefully designed for aesthetic value and plant compatibility, as well

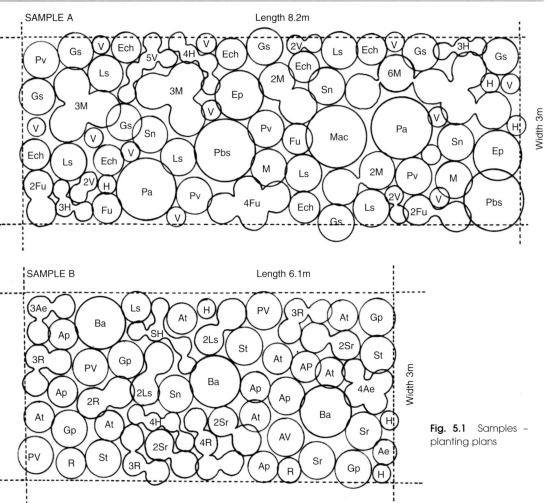

Fig. 5.1 Samples – planting plans

[1] Thompson, P. *The Self-Sustaining Garden*. Batsford, London, 1997.

Fig. 5.2 Samples – plant details

SAMPLE A

ABBREVIATION	PLANT NAME
Pv	*Panicum virgatum*
Sn	*Sorghastrum nutans* 'Indian Steel'
Eph	*Echinacea purpurea*
Ep	*Eupatorium fistulosum* 'Atropurpureum'
Fu	*Filipendula ulmaria*
Gs	*Geranium sylvaticum*
Ls	*Lythrum salicaria*
M	*Monarda* cvs
Pa	*Persicaria amplexicaulis* vars.
Pbs	*Persicaria bistorta* 'Superba'
V	*Valeriana officinalis*
H	*Verbena hastata*
Mac	*Macleaya cordata*
	Camassia quamash scattered in groups of 5-10 at 15-20cm spacings

SAMPLE B

ABBREVIATION	PLANT NAME
Pv	*Panicum virgatum*
Sn	*Sorghastrum nutans* 'Indian Steel'
Ae	*Aster ericoides* vars.
Ap	*Aster puniceus*
At	*Aster turbinellus*
Ba	*Baptisia australis*
Gp	*Geranium phaeum*
Lsp	*Liatris spicata*
R	*Rudbeckia fulgida* var. deamii
St	*Sanguisorba tenuifolia*
Sr	*Solidago rigida*
H	*Verbena hastata*

Total planted area: 200 square metres
Aspect: open, sunny
Soil: deep, fertile, Mesic loam

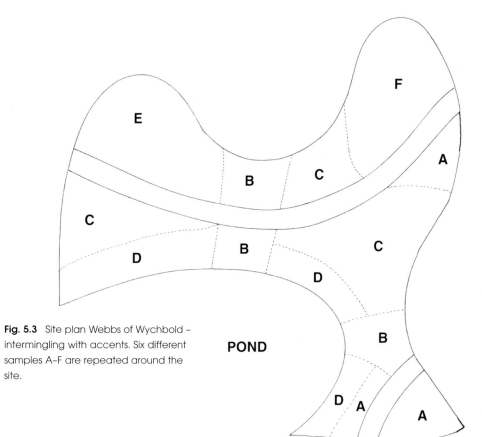

Fig. 5.3 Site plan Webbs of Wychbold – intermingling with accents. Six different samples A–F are repeated around the site.

as suitability to the site and growing conditions. Some plants, such as *Verbena hastata* are in small groups of no more than four or five plants, whereas others, such as *Geranium sylvaticum*, are dotted throughout. This gives the effect of plants intermingling, as they would in nature, with some in clusters and others as singletons. Larger plants, such as

Macleaya cordata, are used as accents.

In the whole area of 200 m² six different samples are used, with each being repeated around the site (Fig. 5.3). The samples have varying emphases on colour and optimum flowering time, but there are also linking plants that run between the samples, unifying the whole area.

Meadow – Random Scattering with Accents

An experiment in meadow planting on the domestic scale has been undertaken over the last five years in a garden in the Sussex Weald. Designer J.S. and consultant, Mike Mullis, have collaborated to produce an enhanced meadow. A sinuous mown path takes the visitor into the centre of the planting, where it enlarges to form a resting place or 'picnic spot'. Seating is placed amongst the flowers, or one can choose to sit on the grass and be surrounded by the planting, which reaches 90cm high in summer (Plate 23).

The seed mix was derived from mainly local plants, but in order to increase biodiversity and wildlife value, plants of Downland and also cultivated origin have been included. The seed was sown into scarifications in the existing lawn grass, because it was anticipated that there would be a flourish of flowers from the dormant seed bank, once the wild plants were freed from the dominance of the grass. Plant plugs were also used to increase the likelihood of successful establishment of flowers such as, *Primula veris* (cowslip), *Lychnis flos-cuculi* (ragged robin) and *Geranium pratense* (meadow cranesbill). The plugs were sown in a random pattern, but positioned carefully with respect to the soil conditions and aspect. For example, the *Primula vulgaris* (primroses) and *Succisa pratensis* (Devil's bit scabious) were concentrated in the shade of the fence, whereas the *Geranium pratense* (meadow cranesbill), *Lychnis flos-cuculi* (ragged robin) and *Silene dioica* (red campion) were placed in the open (Fig. 5.4).

Native shrubs such as *Corylus avellana* and *Euonymous europeaus* were planted in the meadow as accents and also to give structure to the *pointilliste* planting of wild flowers and grasses.

The meadow was mown fortnightly in the first growing season on high blades, in order to weaken the lawn grasses and allow the perennials to establish. Grass cuttings are always removed.

PLANT PLUGS OR 9cm POTS

Stachys officialis (Betony)

Pimpinella saxifraga (Burnet saxifrage)

Primula veris (Cowslip)

Succisa pratensis (Devil's bit scabious)

Genista tinctoria (Dyer's greenwood)

Lotus pedunculatus (Greater bird's foot trefoil)

Centaurea nigra (Lesser knapweed)

Geranium pratense (Meadow cranesbill)

Leucanthemum vulgare (Ox-eye daisy)

Lychnis flos-cuculi (Ragged robin)

Silene dioica (Red campion)

Leontodon hispidus (Rough hawkbit)

HIGH WEALD SEED MIX

DENSITY %	PLANT NAME
10	*Lotus corniculatus* (Bird's foot trefoil)
10	*Centaurea nigra* (Lesser Knapweed)
10	*Ranunculus acris* (Meadow buttercup)
10	*Leucanthemum vulgare* (Ox-eye daisy)
5	*Pimpinella saxifraga* (Burnet saxifrage)
5	*Rumex acetosa* (Common sorrel)
5	*Hypericum perforatum* (Common St. John's wort)
5	*Succisa pratensis* (Devil's bit scabious)
5	*Medicago sativa* (Lucerne) *
5	*Malva moschata* (Musk mallow)
5	*Trifolium pratense* (Red Clover)
5	*Plantago lanceolata* (Ribwort plantain)
5	*Leontodon hispidus* (Rough hawkbit)
5	*Prunella vulgaris* (Self heal)
5	*Achillea millefolium* (Yarrow)
1	*Stachys officinalis* (Betony)
1	*Dactylorhiza fuchsii* (Common spotted orchid)
1	*Primula veris* (Cowslip) #
1	*Galium verum* (Lady's bedstraw) #
1	*Daucus carota* (Wild carrot) #

Downland Origin, * Cultivated Origin

Aspect: Open site
Soil: Fertile, clay

Fig. 5.4 Meadow planting

Coppiced Woodland – Accents and Intermingling

The coppicing of woodland is a traditional process designed to increase the yield of harvested wood. The practice results in a diverse woodland edge community of herbaceous plants and bulbs happy in the semi-shade. The community is a dynamic one as the habitat changes with the years; shade-tolerant plants create a permanent ground cover but when the trees are coppiced the increase in light and warmth encourages biennials and short-lived perennials to colonize the space. As the trees grow back and the canopy develops these transient species die leaving the shade lovers carpeting the ground before the process is repeated. Coppice management represents a means of intimately integrating woody plants with a flowering herbaceous layer and is the naturalistic, dynamic counterpart of the 'mixed border'.

Nigel Dunnett has run trials based on coppicing principles to determine the optimum combination of perennials for such conditions.[2] Even a single tree can be coppiced so these plantings may be adapted for the smallest domestic garden (Plate 24). The accents of the multi-stemmed trees create focal points within the design whilst the groundcover planting intermingles beneath. The dynamism of a naturalistic planting scheme is enhanced by the change in light and shade over the years.

2 Dunnett, N. 'At the Cutting Edge'. *The Garden*, May 2000.

Trees	Planted Perennials	Transients from Seed	Bulbs
EARLY-SEASON COPPICE – cut back herbaceous plants in August and remove cuttings.			
Amelanchier lamarckii	Digitalis ferruginea Geranium psilostemon Geranium sylvaticum	Galium mollugo Hesperis matronalis Lunaria annua Ranunculus acris Silene dioica	
LATE SEASON COPPICE – cut back herbaceous plants in Jan/Feb and remove cuttings (Plate 25).			
Rhus typhina	**For late interest** Aster divaricatus Geranium psilostemon Persicaria amplexicaulis Rudbeckia fulgida var. deamiii **For early interest** (shaded by later perennial growth) Geranium sylvaticum Primula vulgaris		
NATIVE-CHARACTER COPPICE – cut back herbaceous plants in winter and remove cuttings.			
Corylus avellana Fraxinus excelsior	Arum italicum Galium odoratum Melica uniflora Primula vulgaris Ranunculus ficaria Viola odoratum	Bromus ramosus Galium mollugo Lunaria annua Milium effusum Silene dioica	Allium ursinum Anemone nemorosa Hyacinthoides non-scripta Narcissus poeticus (not native) Narcissus poeticus var. recurvus (not native)

Fig. 5.5 Recipes for early season, late season and native coppice planting

Dunnett has trialled several combinations of coppice for early and late season interest. After cultivating the ground and clearing all traces of perennial weeds the bare-root whips are planted at intervals of 1.5–2m. For smaller planting areas and more immediate effect, larger trees up to 1.8m tall may be used. Dunnett's research shows that they establish better than the whips, rooting quickly and putting on strong growth after the initial coppicing. All trees are cut back to near ground level after planting and subsequently cut back at any time from one to five years, depending on the desired ultimate size. The ground cover perennials are planted at random on a 50cm grid and a seed mix of transient woodland edge biennials and perennials is then sown over the whole area. So long as grasses are not included in the seed mix there is no need to keep a clean plant-free area around the base of each tree (Fig. 5.5).

The Small Garden – Natural Dispersion and Intermingling

Lee Heykoop, at her garden in Lincolnshire,[3] creates naturalistic planting schemes on a small scale (Fig. 5.6). Heykoop chooses plants suitable for the soil and then selects with an understanding of performance throughout the year. This together with an aesthetic appreciation of colour and form gives her the plant palette (Fig. 5.7).

The garden is an intimate and sensual experience; gone are traditional axes and focal points. An intricate matrix of small plants underscores simple combinations of larger perennials placed randomly in twos or threes, giving the illusion of having seeded from a larger group. The selection of plants of similar height and flower size allows flowerheads to intermingle and avoids dramatic contrasts.

Heykoop follows the natural dispersion model in her use of the grasses, *Stipa tenuissima*, *Stipa calamagrostis*, and also with the perennial *Achillea* 'Feuerland'. Larger groups of three or more plants give way to twos or threes and then to singletons dispersed through the planting. *Stipa calamagrostis* is used in this way throughout the garden, giving the impression that it has seeded across paths. Heykoop's inclusion of several varieties of stipa and achillea add

---

[3] Dunnett, N. 'Putting Plants First'. *The Garden*, November, 2001.

Fig. 5.6 The small garden (simplified detail) – natural dispersion and intermingling

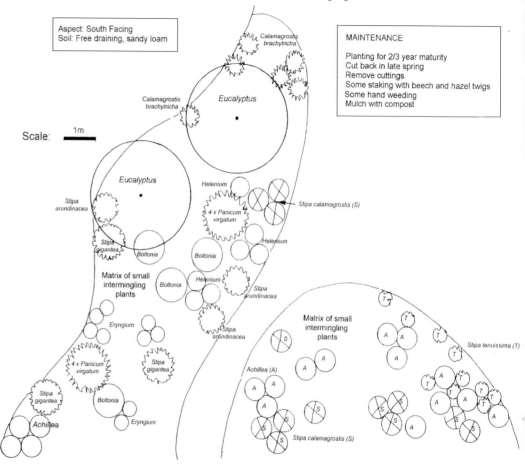

Aspect: South Facing
Soil: Free draining, sandy loam

MAINTENANCE

Planting for 2/3 year maturity
Cut back in late spring
Remove cuttings
Some staking with beech and hazel twigs
Some hand weeding
Mulch with compost

Scale: 1m

interest whilst maintaining the dispersion effect. The natural rhythm of the grasses gives consistency to the design. They flow round the garden linking different areas whilst the larger perennials at the height of their display form visual anchors (Plate 26).

PLANTS SHOWN ON PLAN IMITATING NATURAL DISPERSION	NATURAL HABITAT	INTERMINGLING MATRIX	NATURAL HABITAT[4]
Achillea 'Apfelblüte', 'Feuerland', 'Summerwine' or 'Walther Funcke'	Meadows	Acanthus spinosus	Dry scrub
Boltonia asteroides var. latisquama,	Gravel shores and sandy thickets	Allium cristophii	Well drained soil
Calamagrostis brachytricha	Scrub and forest margins	Asphodeline liburnica	Dry scrub, open woods
Eryngium x tripartitum	Dry, rocky slopes	Aster x frikartii 'Mönch', turbinellus	Scrub, open woods
Helenium 'Rubinzwerg'	Damp meadows	Baptisia australis	Rich soil
Panicum virgatum 'Rehbraun' or 'Rotstrahlbusch'	Prairies, open ground	Centaurea benoistii	Rocky
Stipa tenuissima	Rock slopes, exposed dry grassland	Echinacea purpurea 'Robert Bloom' or 'Leuchstern'	Prairies, dry open woods
Stipa arundinacea	Rich grassland	Eryngium amethystinum or alpinum 'Blue Star'	Rocky meadows
Stipa calamagrostis	Open rocky ground	Euphorbia griffithii 'Dixter'	Clearings and scrub
Stipa gigantea	Open grassland	Geranium 'Ann Folkard' or psilostemon	Scrub, meadows, open forest
		Hemerocallis 'Golden Chimes' or 'Mrs. Hugh Johnson'	Meadows
		Lindelofia longiflora	Open, grassy slopes
		Monarda 'Prärienacht'	Moist woods and scrub
		Nepeta sibirica	Grassland
		Salvia nemorosa 'Ostfriesland', S. var. turkestanica', S. x sylvestris 'Blauhügel' or 'Mainacht'	Rocky slopes
		Scutellaria incana	Open woods, scrub
		Solidaster luteus 'Lemore'	Garden origin
		Verbena bonariensis	Wet fields

Fig. 5.7 The Small Garden – plant selections

---

[4] Philips Roger and Rix Martyn, *The Garden Plant Series – Perennials*. Macmillan, 1994

Natural Dispersion

- Allow self-seeding with ephemeral/ naturalizing planting.
- Give the impression of seeding across paths and boundaries.
- Create the impression of natural dispersion with the use of emergent plants which do not self-seed.[5]
- Use a competitive static plant to prevent a self-seeder from taking over, e.g. aruncus to control self-seeding angelica.[6]

Intermingling/Random Scattering

- These schemes are the most sustainable and the closest to nature.
- Allow plants to self-seed.
- Weed out undesirables.
- Keep fertility low to prevent influx of grasses.
- Create layers of seasonal interest with successional planting.

[5] Pearson, D. See Profile Chapter 6.
[6] Pearson, D. Personal communication, March 2003.

PRACTITIONER PROFILE

KEITH WILEY

Keith Wiley's interest in gardens developed from childhood, when his father allowed him to design and tend his three-acre garden. Although his training was in traditional garden styles and horticulture, his imagination was captured by natural landscapes. He aims to capture the essence of wilderness in all his designs. His work at The Garden House for 25 years developed compositions of different naturalistic schemes that reflected varied natural locations (Plates 27, 28, 29).

Planting Philosophy

Throw the rule book out if you feel so inclined.

Wiley travels all over the world to observe landscapes and plant combinations. Back at The Garden House, he drew on these experiences. The location and ambience of the site that he is designing will often resonate with a landscape seen in the wild and this forms the basis of a design abstracted from nature. His work is not a literal translation of what he sees, rather a 'romanticizing of nature'. He seeks to abstract the 'essence' of a natural landscape and translate it into domestic terms.

If you really believe in a gardening style, stick with it despite the criticisms.

Advice

- Use plants that are suited to the site, but are reminiscent of the plants from the natural landscape that you are evoking. For example, magnolias look like the bare stems and branches of ash trees in winter.
- Plants with narrow leaves often work well in a community, because they allow space for other leaves and they do not cast too much shade. Similarly, plants that have circumscribed root balls that do not spread too much are good in groups.
- Keeping lawns and hedges in immaculate condition, with well-trimmed edges helps to contain and give structure to the informality of naturalistic parts of the garden, especially near the house.
- The structure and shape of the land should be given as much thought as any of the planting. A strong sensual shape invariably looks good all year.
- Prolong the season of interest by designing several washes of colour to take over from one another throughout the year.
- In smaller sites use smaller plants and more bulbs.
- Wiley's particular planting methods are high maintenance; a style for the enthusiast, with time and dedication.

Planting Combinations

- *Verbena bonariensis* with species of aster and miscanthus.
- *Aster novi belgii* with grasses to break up the line of the aster clumps.
- Swiss hay meadow beside an English wild flower meadow.

Contact Details:

Keith Wiley has now left the Garden House, Buckland Monachorum, Devon. He can be contacted on wildsideplants@hotmail.com.

Rather than imitating nature, abstractions are created with the use of planes, blocks and drifts of planting. In such schemes perennials and grasses are selected for their small flowerheads or their resemblance to the wild parent plant, and single species are grouped, often at high densities. The development of the scheme depends on the level of intervention; natural dispersion may be encouraged or self-seeded plants weeded out each year.

Lady Farm – Drifts, Accents and Natural Dispersion[1,2]

The steppe at Lady Farm in Somerset was designed by owner Judy Pearce with the horticulturist Mary Payne. It is approached from above, a rippling mass of *Stipa tenuissima* halted by bright blocks of yellow *Coreopsis verticillata*. Stipa is a very tactile plant and the billowing drifts draw the viewer down and into the planting. As befits a rocky steppe the whole area is mulched with gravel and the drifts of grass wind around the rocks and shingle. *Verbascum olympicum* and varieties of kniphofia, create colourful, vertical accents punctuating the plane beneath. These natural

[1] Rosser, L. 'Steppe this Way'. *The Garden Design Journal*, Autumn, 1998.
[2] Brookes, J. 'Naturally Relaxed'. *The Garden*, September, 2001.

'full-stops' are essential to the design bringing both an element of drama and drawing the eye around the space (Plate 30).

Before planting, all perennial weeds were removed, but in order to keep the soil fertility low, no fertilizers were added. Plants were chosen for their suitability to the dry, rocky conditions and matched for their competitiveness; any subsequently found to be too vigorous, for example *Artemisia ludoviciana* 'Silver Queen', were removed.

The exuberant dynamism of the planting is a result of encouraging self-seeding; there was no formal planting plan and the perennials were laid out in clumps and *Stipa tenuissima* dotted in the gaps. Over time the grass formed drifts around the more static perennials and shrub-like planting and the verbascum and kniphofia dispersed naturally throughout the steppe. As a result the gravel and shingle in some areas has all but disappeared under the dense planting. This is a matter of preference; if sparse drifts in gravel are a requirement, some judicious hand weeding is necessary to remove the stipa and verbascum seedlings (Figs. 6.1, 6.2).

Fig. 6.1 Lady Farm (simplified detail) drifts, accents and natural dispersion

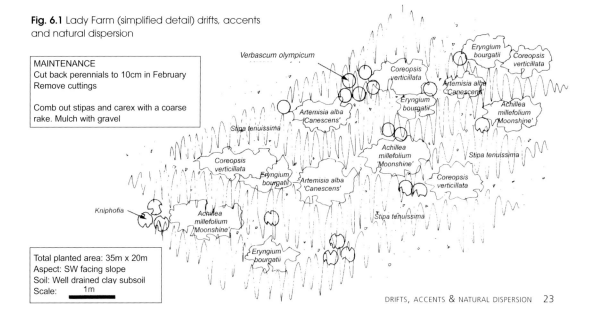

MAINTENANCE
Cut back perennials to 10cm in February
Remove cuttings

Comb out stipas and carex with a coarse rake. Mulch with gravel

Total planted area: 35m x 20m
Aspect: SW facing slope
Soil: Well drained clay subsoil
Scale: 1m

PLANTS SHOWN ON PLAN	DENSITY/sq m	NATURAL HABITAT
Achillea millefolium 'Moonshine'	7	Dry grassland
Artemisia alba 'Canescens'	9	Dry, open ground
Coreopsis verticillata	5	Clearings on dry soil, thickets
Eryngium bourgatii	9	Dry, rocky ground
Kniphofia species	Dispersed	Well drained
Stipa tenuissima	Dotted	Rocky slopes, exposed dry grassland
Verbascum olympicum	Dispersed	Dry scrub

UNDERPLANTING FOR EARLY SUMMER

Allium moly	Clumps and dotted	Dry, stony
Euphorbia myrsinites	7	Rocky slopes
Euphorbia polychroma	7	Wood and scrub
Tulipa tarda	Clumps and dotted	Dry, stony

OTHER STEPPE PLANTS AT LADY FARM

Berberis thunbergii f.atropurpurea 'Atropurpurea Nana'	7	Scrub, forest margins
Carex comans (bronze form)	5	Damp grassland
Carex flagellifera	5	Damp, open areas
Oenothera macrocarpa	7	Dry, gravel
Stipa gigantea	3	Open grassland

Fig. 6.2 Lady Farm – plant selections

Fig. 6.3 Lady Farm – Planes (detail – right). For colour representation, see Plate 31.

Aspect: West
Soil: Well drained, clay subsoil

PLANTING DENSITIES/square metre:
Achillea 'Fanal' 9
Calamagrostis x acutiflora
 'Karl Foerster' 7
Salvia x sylvestris 'Mainacht' 9

MAINTENANCE
Cut back to 10cm in February
Remove cuttings
Mulch with bark after planting

Lady Farm – Planes

Alongside the steppe planting at Lady Farm is an extensive area of prairie; bold exuberant blocks of perennials and grasses, in some cases with flower heads intermingling and in others retaining their own space (Plate 31). Sections of the prairie demonstrate the use of planes in the strong horizontal and vertical forms of their planting. Salvia x sylvestris 'Mainacht' creates upright purple accents in front of the flat, fiery flowerheads of Achillea 'Fanal' and this is backed by the massed verticals of Calamagrostis x acutiflora 'Karl Foerster' (Fig. 6.3). The drama is maintained even into winter when the low sunlight creates silhouettes of the dead flowerheads.

Grasses, such as miscanthus and calamagrostis with their distinctive structure, are obvious can-didates for such planting and the contrasting horizontal flowerheads of the achillea serve to emphasize the three-dimensionality of the composition. Such designs are possible on both large and small scales and rely for their impact on a reduced plant palette of two or three species with a neutral backdrop of shrubs, clipped evergreens, hard landscaping such as water and rock or even the sky.

Plate 17. Sussex chalk meadow at Cuckmere Haven shows random scattering of dots of colour. Photo: Juliet Sargeant

Plate 18. Ferns create accents in the understorey of this managed woodland in the Yorkshire Dales. Photo: Catherine Heatherington

Plate 19. A horizontal plane of reeds on the Scottish island of Islay stretches to the horizon. Photo: Catherine Heatherington

Plate 20. Native planting on rocks in the Yorkshire Dales creates a pattern of blocks of green. Photo: Catherine Heatherington

Plate 21. Noël Kingsbury uses large 'back-of-border' plants such as eupatorium to create accents. In this planting on a steep bank the pink flowerheads intermingling with the white of the *Cimicifuga ramosa*, tower above head-height.
Design: Noël Kingsbury
Photo: Juliet Sargeant,

Plate 22. Accents of *Calamagrostis x acutiflora* 'Karl Foerster' emerge from geraniums at Cowley Manor, Gloucestershire, Summer 2002.
Design: Noël Kingsbury
Photo: Juliet Sargeant

Plate 23. A mown path meandering through the meadow in a small Sussex garden opens into a seating area amongst the planting.
Design & Photo: Juliet Sargeant

Plate 24. Coppiced hazel with the intermingling of native British planting in a small garden.
Design & Photo: Nigel Dunnett

Plate 26. A late summer planting in a Lincolnshire garden showing natural dispersion of *Calamagrostis brachytricha* and *Stipa calamagrostis* through an intermingling matrix of small plants. *Helenium* 'Rubinzwerg' in the foreground.
Design & Photo: Lee Heykoop

Plate 25. Accents of coppiced *Rhus typhina* with *Rudbeckia fulgida* var. *deamii* in autumn.
Design & Photo: Nigel Dunnett

Plate 27. In his 'South African Garden' Keith Wiley has used not only South African plants, but also those that evoke the sense of that landscape, whilst being suited to a temperate, maritime climate. The Garden House, Devon, Summer 2002.
Design: Keith Wiley
Photo: Juliet Sargeant

Plates 28 & 29. At The Garden House a Swiss hay meadow is planted beside a traditional English meadow. This increases the variety and
longevity of summer colour, Summer 2002.
Design: Keith Wiley
Photo: Juliet Sargeant

An Oxfordshire Garden – Drifts, Accents and Blocks

This one and a half acre garden was designed by Tom Stuart-Smith as part of a large private garden. The area stands above the surrounding countryside, and by using only two walls Stuart-Smith has created a sheltered, south-facing space opening out to the agrarian landscape beyond. The rectilinear fields are reflected in the geometry of the design and the scale of the open countryside is echoed in the vast planting beds, which are crossed by smaller, informal pathways.

These paths curve into and around the organic masses of planting, softening the geometry of the design (Plate 32). The drifts of *Salvia* 'Blauhügel' are interplanted in places, with grasses and perennials such as *Asphodeline liburnica*, *Stachys byzantina* 'Silver Carpet', and *Sedum telephium* 'Matrona' (Fig. 6.4). Masses of *Festuca amesthystina* have *Dianthus carthusianorum* and *Eryngium bourgatii* planted through them. Vertical accents of yew and hornbeam punctuate the waves of planting which undulate in both the horizontal and the vertical planes.

The original soil on the site is Ironstone Brash, heavy clay. The site was previously rough grass and it required extensive preparation. Large stones were removed and copious amounts of mushroom compost and sharp sand added. Close planting densities were used for quick effect and watering points incorporated.

Aster x frikartii 'Mönch'

Salvia 'Blaughügel'

Sedum 'Matrona'

Artemisia 'Powis Castle'

Nepata 'Walker's Low'

Stachys 'Silver Carpet'

Fig. 6.4 An Oxfordshire Garden – drifts, accents and blocks (simplified detail)

Total planted area: 60mx60m
Aspect: open, sunny, south-facing

Soil: heavy clay prepared with sharp sand and mushroom compost

PLANTING DENSITIES/square metre

Aster x frikartii 'Mönch'	7
Artemisia 'Powis Castle'	3
Nepeta racemosa 'Walker's Low'	7
Salvia x sylvestris 'Blauhügel'	7
Sedum telephium 'Matrona'	7
Stachys byzantina 'Silver Carpet'	5

MAINTENANCE

Annual mulch with composted bark
Weeding by hand and selective removal of self-seeded plants and rampant types
Irrigation as required
Plants left for winter effect and removed as they become unsightly

The garden is weeded by a skilled team that can make the vital judgements needed to allow a dynamic interplay between nature and the original design. They are constantly deciding whether to remove a plant that has become too rampant and whether to allow a self-seeded plant to stay. The garden is watered if necessary and the watering point system allows for the flexibility to water one area and not another. The plants are cut back only when they become unsightly, because the grass seeds and structural flower heads are part of the design; intended to prolong the season of interest from the main flourish in June and July, through to the winter months. The last to be cut back are the miscanthus, usually late in January. Fertilizer is not necessary with the rich clay soil, but the whole garden is mulched each spring.

Pensthorpe Waterfowl Park – Blocks[3]

Piet Oudolf designed the 0.5 hectare of naturalistic planting at Pensthorpe Waterfowl Park in spring 2000. His use of species and varieties of perennials that most closely resemble wild plants, together with grasses, enables Oudolf to create schemes that evoke rather than copy nature. Although habitat is important, Oudolf does not let this restrict his choice of plants and stresses the importance of texture, form and flower structure. In the tradition of Karl Foerster, Oudolf has bred plants at his nursery in The Netherlands, selecting varieties with a long flowering season which stand up without staking. He prefers species with small flowerheads rather than large or double forms. Most crucial is the requirement for the seed and flower heads to keep their structure throughout the winter. At Pensthorpe the grasses are allowed to stand until the early spring but the wet maritime climate determines that the perennials are often cut back in late autumn.

Oudolf creates large, high-density blocks of single plants which are then repeated through the design (Figs. 6.5, 6.6). The large number of plants per square metre ensures that the display is dramatic even in the first year. This repetition of colour and form gives a unity to the planting and draws the eye around and into the garden. Plants do not intermingle and there are

[3] Heatherington, C. 'Pause for Pensthorpe'. *The Garden Design Journal*, February, 2001.

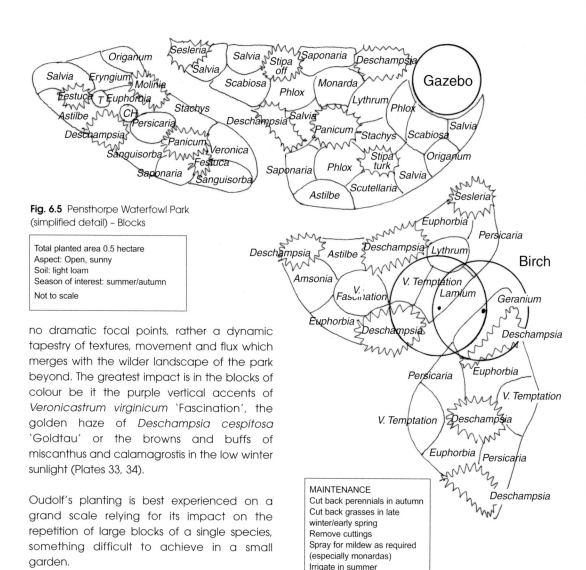

Fig. 6.5 Pensthorpe Waterfowl Park (simplified detail) – Blocks

Total planted area 0.5 hectare
Aspect: Open, sunny
Soil: light loam
Season of interest: summer/autumn

Not to scale

no dramatic focal points, rather a dynamic tapestry of textures, movement and flux which merges with the wilder landscape of the park beyond. The greatest impact is in the blocks of colour be it the purple vertical accents of *Veronicastrum virginicum* 'Fascination', the golden haze of *Deschampsia cespitosa* 'Goldtau' or the browns and buffs of miscanthus and calamagrostis in the low winter sunlight (Plates 33, 34).

Oudolf's planting is best experienced on a grand scale relying for its impact on the repetition of large blocks of a single species, something difficult to achieve in a small garden.

MAINTENANCE
Cut back perennials in autumn
Cut back grasses in late winter/early spring
Remove cuttings
Spray for mildew as required (especially monardas)
Irrigate in summer

PLANT NAME	DENSITY/ sq m	NATURAL HABITAT	PLANT NAME	DENSITY/ sq m	NATURAL HABITAT
Amsonia tabernaemontana var. *salicifolia*	7	Damp, grassy	*Saponaria x lempergii* 'Max Frei'	9	Rock and scrub
Astilbe chinensis var *taquettii* 'Purpurlanze'	7	Damp woods, shady streams	*Scabiosa japonica var, alpina*	9	Dry meadows and rocky slopes
Chaerophyllum hirsutum 'Roseum'	7	Grassy, scrub	*Scutellaria incana*	7	Open woods, scrub
Eryngium alpinum 'Blue Star'	9	Rocky, subalpine meadows	*Stachys macrantha* 'Superba'	7	Rocky slopes and scrub
Euphorbia griffithii 'Dixter'	7	Clearings and scrub	*Stachys monieri* 'Hummelo'	7	Rocky slopes
Geranium phaeum	7	Meadows, woods	*Thalictrum aquilegifolium*	7	Meadows
Geranium sanguineum	7	Sunny, grassy, scrub	*Veronica spicata* 'Spitzentraum'	7	Dry meadows and steppe
Geranium x oxonianum 'Rebecca Moss'	7	Woods and scrub	*Veronicastrum virginicum* 'Fascination'	7	Moist meadows, wood, scrub
Lamium orvala	7	Scrub and woodland edge	*Veronicastrum virginicum* 'Temptation'	7	Moist meadows, wood, scrub
Lythrum virgatum	7	Marshes	**GRASSES**[4]		
Monarda 'Mohawk'	7	Scrub and wood edges	*Deschampsia cespitosa* 'Goldtau'	5	Boggy, poorly drained grasslands
Origanum pulchellum 'Rosenkuppel'	9	Rocky scrub	*Festuca mairei*	1	Rocky slopes
Persicaria amplexicaulis 'Rosea'	3	Scrub and stream edge	*Molinia caerulea*	5	Moorlands, damp peaty areas
Persicaria amplexicaulis 'Firedance'	3	Moist scrub, mountain meadows	*Panicum virgatum* 'Rehbraun'	5	Prairies, open ground
Phlox maculata 'Delta'	7	Meadows, marshes, woods	*Panicum virgatum* 'Strictum'	3	Prairies, open ground
Salvia officinalis 'Würzburg'	3	Rocky slopes	*Sesleria nitida*	5	Sunny
Salvia verticillata 'Purple Rain'	7	Rocky slopes	*Stipa offneri*	7	Dry grassland
Sanguisorba menziesii	7	Meadows, wet grass	*Stipa turkestanica*	7	Stony scree
Sanguisorba 'Tanna'	5	Meadows and wet grass			

Fig. 6.6 Plants used at Pensthorpe, their planting densities and natural habitats. In the planting schemes, complementary varieties are sometimes intermingled, and smaller groups of 3–5 plants inserted. Block sizes vary from approx. 4 to 10 square metres.

[4] Grounds, Roger, *Ornamental Grasses*. Pelham Books, London, 1979. A later edition is mentioned in the bibliography.

Accents

- Select strong, long-lasting vertical forms with a good winter seed-head or silhouette.
- Select plants which will not self-seed, unless a natural dispersion model is required.

Planes

- If designing a monoculture or with a limited palette more competitive plants may be selected to prevent seeding of other plants into the group.
- Use a limited palette of perennials and grasses with strong horizontal and vertical forms.

Drifts

- Choose non-naturalizing plants to keep the shapes of the drifts.
- Or allow seeding and weed out any plants in the 'wrong' place.
- Create static blocks for the seeding plants to drift around.
- Select plants for the static forms which do not allow the ephemerals to seed into them, e.g. ruta, miscanthus and santolina.[5]
- Consider the winter form of the static blocks.
- By considering heights, the drifts can be made to undulate in both the horizontal and vertical planes.

Blocks

- Use non-naturalizing species in high densities in large groups.
- Select compatible plants of similar competitiveness to allow for high-density planting.
- Achieve rhythm by repeating colours and forms over a large-scale planting.

---

[5] Pearson, D. Personal communication, March 2003.

PRACTITIONER PROFILE

DAN PEARSON

Dan Pearson has been interested in plants since childhood. He studied at Wisley and the Edinburgh Botanic Gardens and obtained a Diploma in Horticulture from Kew Gardens, London. While studying he won scholarships to travel to the mountains of Northern Spain, the Himalayas and to Israel where he developed a fascination for the balance and aesthetic qualities of naturally occurring plant communities.

Planting Philosophy

You have to be patient – this isn't an exact science. Sometimes you have to let it go to understand the way the plants truly respond to their location.

Pearson's in-depth understanding of plants is his starting point and with this knowledge he selects combinations that he knows will work in a particular situation. An understanding of the site is therefore crucial, both in terms of a practical knowledge and an awareness of the sense of place, the 'genius loci'. The clients' requirements are also paramount, and Pearson will only create an ephemeral planting scheme if the client wants to be involved in its development and maintenance. For public spaces he prefers to create drifts of naturalistic planting which are static in their shape over time; they do not self-seed or run.

It has to be practical or it won't work.

Advice

- Always 'read the site first' to understand the soil, microclimate, conditions, aspect, habitat and locality.
- Aim for a scheme which requires no staking, little feeding, spraying or watering after it has established. Mulch after planting and after cutting back in early spring.
- Balance ephemeral, self-seeding plants with static forms and combinations such as clump-forming perennials that do not need dividing. For example miscanthus, santolina and kniphofia. The proportion of 20% ephemeral to 80% static works well.
- Choose compatible plants of equal competitiveness to enable planting at high density in small gardens.
- Use emergent, semi-transparent plants en masse to give the appearance of spontaneity, e.g. umbellifers like *Foeniculum vulgare* 'Purpureum' (Bronze Fennel), grasses such as *Molinia* subsp. *arundinacea* 'Transparent', and *Verbena bonariensis*.

Planting Combinations

To create successional schemes, begin with ground cover plants to protect the soil and add emergent perennials to give a series of layers, (Plates 35, 36, 37).

Gardens open to the public

Althorp, Northamptonshire.

Contact Details: Dan Pearson Studio, 80c Battersea Rise, London SW11 1EH
Tel: 020 7924 2518. Fax: 020 7924 2523
E-mail: danpearson@macunlimited.net

7 PRACTICAL ISSUES: IMPLEMENTATION & MAINTENANCE

In Chapter 3 consideration was given to the importance of humans in the design of naturalistic gardens. The design must be pleasing and it must motivate people to commit time and effort to maintaining it, especially the planting. It is essential for a designer to have a clear idea of how much time, money and horticultural skill is available to implement and maintain a garden. After a couple of growing seasons any garden, no matter how well designed, is only as good as its maintenance. The resources available will fundamentally affect the choice of plants, their combinations and the course that the whole design takes.

In earlier chapters naturalism has been seen as a spectrum of design ideologies; from those with a strong emphasis on design to those that mimic natural habitats and will only incorporate native species. Maintenance of these gardens follows a similar spectrum from regimes that use largely traditional horticultural methods to those that reject all artificial methods and seek to garden in harmony with natural processes.

This chapter will outline the issues involved in implementing and maintaining a naturalistic garden, so that designers can assess for themselves where they stand and which methods best suit their designs. The reader will see that in the face of reality, often a pragmatic approach is taken. A designer creates a design that can be kept looking good by the regular attention of the people available, bearing in mind their level of horticultural skill. Where the design stands along the spectrum of naturalism should depend as much on the practicalities of maintenance as on the ideology of designer and client.

The practical considerations of the site vary widely, from a small domestic plot with a highly skilled professional gardener to a large urban reclamation project with an army of enthusiastic, but unskilled volunteers. Three main factors to assess carefully are: the size of the plot, the time available for maintenance and how that is distributed over the year, and the horticultural skill and experience of the gardeners.

Plants must survive if a planting scheme is to remain attractive, and for this there are several general requirements. These are part of any maintenance plan. Each plant will require adequate sunlight, moisture, nutrients, air circulation around leaves and roots, protection from the elements and also from pests and diseases. The specific requirements of each type of plant will vary and therein lies a fundamental difference between 'intensive' and 'extensive' gardening.

---

[1] Thompson, P. *The Self-Sustaining Garden.* Batsford, London, 1997.

Traditional horticultural methods are intensive; the individual requirements of each plant are met by digging, hoeing, staking, fertilizing, watering, weeding, splitting and pest control. And their requirements are very varied, because traditionally plants are combined for their artistic merits rather than their ecological compatibility. If plants from diverse habitats are placed in the same bed, then of course they must be tended individually and intensively. But, paradoxically, traditional soil care aims to homogenize, not only the soil profile on a particular site, but also the soil from one region to another. The 'ideal'[1] soil that the keen gardener aspires to is a homogenous mix of dark, crumbly moisture-retentive, but well-drained loam. And this will be the case, whether the site is in the Scottish Highlands, or the east coast of America. This ideal soil is deliberately kept very rich in moisture and nutrients, so as to reduce the need for the plants to compete.

At the opposite pole lies extensive maintenance, and the clearest example of this is the traditional hay meadow. The soil is not cultivated from one year to the next and plants have to compete to fulfil their requirements. The whole area is treated by a simultaneous cut once a year, and those plants that succumb to drought or disease are not nurtured back to health, nor replaced. The plants that survive have adapted to the conditions: the local rainfall, the soil profile, the elements, the competition from other plants and the farming regime. A modern example of the application of extensive techniques to the garden situation is sustainable planting. This has been described in detail in Chapter 3.

An established meadow requires low maintenance, and it is options such as this that have attracted many people to the naturalistic style. But naturalism is a broad umbrella and in fact some gardens of this kind still need very high maintenance.

Garden designers develop implementation and maintenance strategies that are a combination of the various techniques available. They choose the methods that best fit the situation, the client's wishes, their own ethos and the resources available. The following are the main factors that need to be considered in designing a maintenance regime; at each step there are various options available.

Perennial Weeds

It is essential to clear the site of perennial weeds before planting. When preparing a plot, hand-weeding is extremely labour-intensive and mechanical rotavation does not remove the roots. Many designers resort to using a systemic weedkiller such as glyphosate, which selectively kills broad-leaved plants and degenerates on contact with the soil. An area can be sprayed completely or the weeds individually spot-treated. If time allows the ground can be left under black plastic for one or two seasons. Unfortunately, these methods will leave the bank of seeds in the soil untouched and when light reaches them they germinate. This is one argument against digging, because it brings weed seeds to the surface to germinate. However, this can be used to the gardener's advantage; an area can be cleared of existing weeds, dug over, left and then the newly germinated seedlings can be treated before they can set their own seed. Spreading a mulch of 150mm of sand also cuts back weed growth[2]. Complete removal of the topsoil is another option that can be considered if an area is to become meadow.

Once a planting is established, an area can be regularly hoed or hand-weeded, as traditionally practised, or plants can be spot-treated with glyphosate. It is also possible to overspray early-growing weeds with glyphosate in winter, when the planted perennials are dormant.[3] The design of the planting will affect the impact that weeds have; close planting allows the plants to quickly form a covering to shade out weeds, and in some instances annuals are used to cover bare soil while perennials establish. It is also true that the more naturalistic the style of planting, the better the occasional weed is hidden in the mass of planting. Conversely, a stray weed is easily noticed in a highly designed bed of planting blocks or rows.

Organic Matter and Soil Improvement

The high nutrient levels and optimum moisture-retaining capacity created by traditional gardening practices allow a wide range of plants to be grown to maximum size and visual impact, with a minimum of competition between them. Sustainable gardening in its purest form advocates little or no disruption of the soil profile with digging. If organic matter is essential, then it is laid on the surface of the soil, to be incorporated gradually by the natural action of worms and bacteria. Plants are then chosen that are adapted to thrive in that particular soil; there is no need to alter it.

Fertilizers

Traditional planting design groups plants of one type together, therefore an area of soil will rapidly become depleted of the particular nutrients used by that plant. The competition would be intense, but for the efforts of the gardener, who repeatedly replenishes the nutrients with fertilizers. In sustainable systems, there will be several plant types in any one area of garden, each with different requirements. This is far more efficient, using all the available resources.

Mulching

Mulching is very important for the efficient use of resources in the garden. A mulch is a layer of organic and/or inorganic material laid over the surface of the soil. It serves to retain moisture in

[2] Dunnett, N. Seminar for The Society of Garden Designers, Kew, March 2003.
[3] Dunnett, N. and Hitchmough, J. Conference at the University of Sheffield, January 2003.

the soil and to suppress the germination and growth of weeds. If the mulch is organic, it has the additional advantage of rotting down, which improves the texture and water-retaining capacity of the soil, and it also releases nutrients as it decomposes. In some sustainable systems, the dead plants that are cut back can be used to mulch the soil, retaining moisture and suppressing weeds. This is usually done as late as possible in order to keep the seed heads and grasses over winter. They not only provide structure and visual interest, but also valuable food and habitats for wildlife.

Slug Predation

Unfortunately, slugs are also wildlife and this is one of the major difficulties facing gardeners in temperate climates. The relatively mild winters and long warm springs allow slugs to predate the soft, fleshy growth of plants as they emerge. Dunnett and Hitchmough have found that by cutting back the perennials earlier in the season and removing the cuttings they greatly reduce the slug grazing,[4] but of course, they are also reducing the advantages for other animals and insects.

Planting

The importance of choosing the right plants for the conditions on the site has already been discussed, as has the contrast between traditional monocultural groups and the complex communities in sustainable methods. Spacing of the

plants is also an important consideration. Traditional methods seek to grow each plant to its maximum size; each is nurtured as an individual specimen with all the space that it requires. This space and the tall, soft structure promoted by generous fertilizing, often results in the need for staking. In nature, plants knit together and support each other physically.[5] The spacing in sustainable gardens is much closer than traditionally seen and therefore, the plants are often smaller and less blousy. This lends itself to the aim of a naturalistic aesthetic. There is no need to divide plants every few years in a sustainable system, because shifts in the composition of the planting occur naturally over time. No one plant is indispensable and many will be crowded out as others become dominant. Occasionally a plant may become particularly rampant, threatening to take over completely and destroy the carefully designed biodiversity, and judicious selective weeding may be necessary.

Irrigation

If drought-resistant plants are chosen for drought-prone sites, there should be little need for regular irrigation. Plants may require watering in the initial stage, while their roots are developing and while they grow to cover the surface of the ground, but once established this will not be needed. If the plants have developed a tight network, the occasional loss to drought or

disease can be sustained. In Beth Chatto's dry, gravel garden the plants are chosen for suitability to an area with the lowest rainfall in Britain.[6] Initially the soil was improved with tonnes of farmyard manure. After planting the whole area was mulched with a thick layer of gravel and the garden now is never watered. In this garden the planting design is mainly clumps and drifts, but close attention to plant suitability and soil preparation has resulted in a very successful low-maintenance garden.

KEY POINTS

- Assess the resources available, both in the short term for implementation and long term for maintenance.
- Assess the impact on the site of the various methods in terms of ethos, but also in terms of the effect on the future maintenance.
- Consider these issues early in the design process, so that the planting chosen suits the resources, the site and ethos of client and designer.

[4] Dunnett, N. and Hitchmough, J. Conference at the University of Sheffield, January 2003.

[5] Wiley, K. Personal interview, January 2003.
[6] Chatto, B. *The Gravel Garden*. Frances Lincoln, London, 1999.

8 THE DESIGN PERSPECTIVE

Imposing a Geometry

A frequent criticism of the design characteristics of naturalistic planting is that they are only suitable for rural areas or wildlife gardens. Although the historical development of such schemes has tended towards organic beds, winding paths and random planting in gravel this need not be the only approach.

Mark Brown's meadow at La Berquerie in Normandy is arranged on a rectilinear grid; mown paths follow the lines of fruit trees running between the twenty rectangular beds of grasses and perennials (Plate 38). This benefits the trees, reducing competition next to the trunk and enables the visitor to walk through the meadow from all directions. The beds are a mass of intermingling plants allowed to self-seed at will, although Brown is on hand to weed out or move undesirables. The unexpected overlaying of a grid on a seemingly natural planting heightens the tension between the 'man-made' and wild and can easily be replicated in small-scale gardens.

Tom Stuart-Smith's garden discussed in Chapter 6 is also based on a strictly geometrical design (Plate 39). Upon entering the walled garden through the main gateway, the eye of the viewer is taken dramatically down a straight line and out into the fields beyond. The path is flanked by drifts of grasses and perennials that echo the colours and forms of the landscape. Similar drama is created by the straight rill that crosses the plateau of undulating planting and leads the eye to a horizontal plane of still water. By moving around the garden along the paths that criss-cross the vast planting masses, one is able to wander more casually into and around the plants, appreciating their detail from every angle. The relaxed curves soften the geometry of the layout, and all the time, this underlying structure is maintained in its three-dimensional form by clipped yew hedges and pleached hornbeams.

Brita von Schoenaich and Tim Rees's use of perennials and grasses as bedding plants pushes the boundaries of accepted naturalistic planting. In a spring and summer scheme for Tate Britain they created strictly linear planting strips of randomized lengths, determined by the throw of a dice (Plates 51 & 52). The plant palette is restricted to six flowering perennials and the intermingling of small flowerheads in the final display gives a naturalistic feel to the composition.

Creating a Backdrop

In nature meadows, verges, moorland and reedbeds merge with the background of hedges, fields, woods and mountains, and historically, naturalistic designs in rural sites have depended on such natural features.

Town gardens are usually enclosed keeping the eye within the space. When using naturalistic planting in an urban space, the designer should consider a more formal backdrop. Clipped hedging such as yew or box create a framework to contain the planting as seen in Christopher Lloyd's meadow at Great Dixter (Plate 43) and Piet Oudolf's garden in The Netherlands (Plates 2 & 41). The buttress-like forms may be geometric, linking with the urban architecture or, in more rural settings, clipped into mounds and organic forms mimicking rolling hills.

Within smaller gardens a wall serves as a solid backdrop contrasting with the ephemeral planting and bringing a moment of stillness in the sea of movement. The positioning of the wall can be exploited to make full use of light and shadow with low sunlight or artificial lighting casting shadows from adjacent planting across the surface.

The simplest backdrop is created as it is in nature with shrubs and trees. These may be native or exotic plants dependent on the effect required. In this case it is not contrast that is important, but rather a structural framework for the planting. Mark Brown's Japanese woodland at La Berquerie (Plate 42) exemplifies this approach. A

Plate 31. The lines of *Calamagrostis x acutiflora* 'Karl Foerster', *Salvia x sylvestris* 'Mainacht' and *Achillea* 'Fanal' create contrasting horizontal and vertical planes, Summer 2002.
Design: Judy Pearce and Mary Payne
Photo: Catherine Heatherington

Plate 30. *Stipa tenuissima* drifts around accents of *Verbascum olympicum* and kniphofia in the steppe planting at Lady Farm, near Bristol, Summer 2002.
Design: Judy Pearce and Mary Payne
Photo: Catherine Heatherington

Plate 32. In this large walled garden Tom Stuart-Smith employs a combination of naturalistic design techniques. Large drifts of *Salvia x sylvestris* 'Blauhügel' and masses of *Festuca amethystina* are broken up and interplanted with perennials for colour and form. Larger yews and hornbeams create sculptural accents, October 2002.
Design: Tom Stuart-Smith
Photo: Juliet Sargeant

Plate 33. The repetition of blocks of *Astilbe chinensis* var. *taquetti* 'Purpurlanze' and *Deschampsia cespitosa* creates a rhythm in the planting at the 0.5 hectare site of Pensthorpe Waterfowl Park, Norfolk, June 2000.
Design: Piet Oudolf
Photo: Catherine Heatherington

Plate 34. The similar forms of *Astilbe chinensis* var. *taquetti* 'Purpurlanze' and *Veronicastrum virginicum* 'Fascination' are planted in large harmonizing colour blocks at Pensthorpe Waterfowl Park, Norfolk, June 2000.
Design: Piet Oudolf
Photo: Catherine Heatherington

Three images of intermingling naturalistic planting using mainly exotic plants in Dan Pearson's own garden.
Photos: Huw Morgan

Plate 36. *Eryngium agavifolium,* and *Dierama pulcherrimum.*

Plate 35. *Digitalis ferruginea* and *Stipa barbata* in the foreground. *Veronicastrum virginicum* 'Fascination' to the rear.

Plate 37. *Geranium* 'Patricia', *Hemerocallis* 'Stafford', *Stipa arundinacea* and *Crocosmia* 'Lucifer'.

Plate 38. The traditional geometry of this old Normandy Orchard has been used as a template for a new meadow garden, July 2003.
Design: Mark Brown
Photo: Juliet Sargeant

Plate 40. Drifts of woodland planting contrast with the simple geometry of this still pool in Tom Stuart-Smith's garden for the Chelsea Flower Show, 2003. Plants include the lime-green
Tellima grandiflora running through densely planted *Hesperis matronalis* and *Iris sibirica* beneath *Cornus kousa* var. *chinensis*.
Design: Tom Stuart-Smith

Plate 39. Tom Stuart-Smith's plateau of still water creates a large reflective plane echoing the fields beyond, October 2002
Design: Tom Stuart-Smith
Photo: Juliet Sargeant

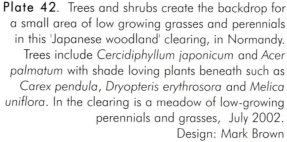

Plate 42. Trees and shrubs create the backdrop for a small area of low growing grasses and perennials in this 'Japanese woodland' clearing, in Normandy. Trees include *Cercidiphyllum japonicum* and *Acer palmatum* with shade loving plants beneath such as *Carex pendula*, *Dryopteris erythrosora* and *Melica uniflora*. In the clearing is a meadow of low-growing perennials and grasses, July 2002.
Design: Mark Brown
Photo: Catherine Heatherington

Plate 41. The dense living buttresses in Piet Oudolf's garden contrast with the ephemeral *Stipa tenuissima*, Summer 2001.
Design: Piet Oudolf
Photo: Catherine Heatherington

Plate 44. Long before planting, the topography of The Garden House, Devon was altered in order to create an undulating landscape opening to views of the valley beyond, Summer 2002
Design: Keith Wiley
Photo: Juliet Sargeant

Plate 43. Vertical blocks of hedging at Great Dixter, E. Sussex form a solid backdrop for the horizontal plane of the meadow in the foreground, June 2002.
Design: Christopher Lloyd
Photo: Juliet Sargeant

Plate 47. The simple colour combination of *Foeniculum vulgare* 'Purpureum' and *Lychnis coronaria* 'Alba' in this intermingling planting links with the colours in the Normandy vernacular architecture, July 2002.
Design: Mark Brown
Photo: Catherine Heatherington

Plate 45. The sandstone coping around this terrace leads the eye to the agrarian landscape where distant tree forms are mirrored by topiary within the garden.
Design: Tom Stuart-Smith
Photo: Juliet Sargeant, October 2002

Plate 46. A plane of fine-textured random planting offsets the simplicity of modern buildings as shown in this meadow next to a school.
Photo: Nigel Dunnett

Plate 48. The gardens for the Westonbirt International Festival 2002 were sited in an open field at Westonbirt Arboretum, Gloucestershire. By using *Calamagrostis x acutiflora* 'Karl Foerster' Catherine Heatherington has blurred the boundary between the meadow grasses and the designed space. The undulating lines of a long bench give structure to the middle ground, Summer 2002.

Design & Photo: Catherine Heatherington

Plate 49. At the Barnes Wetland Centre, London, Arne Maynard has made sculptural use of log pile habitats to create a middle ground within the natural planting, May 2001.
Design: Arne Maynard
Photo: Juliet Sargeant

Plate 50. There is a no formal boundary between Derek Jarman's garden and the shingle beach at Dungeness, Kent. As one nears the small fisherman's hut the plants, such as *Crambe maritima* and *Centranthus ruber*, coalesce to create the garden space. Within and between these plants Jarman has created informal paths and resting places, June 2002.
Design: Derek Jarman
Photo: Juliet Sargeant

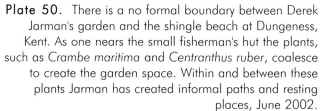

Plate 51. The linear layout of the bedding scheme as determined by the throw of a dice can clearly be seen in this photograph of planting at Tate Britain, London.

Design & Photo: Schoenaich Rees

Plate 52. Later in the season the blocks of colour appear naturalistic due to the delicate forms of the plants and the small flowerheads.
Design & Photo: Schoenaich Rees

meadow of grasses and low-growing perennials is planted in a clearing surrounded by acers, viburnums and cercidophylums. The trees provide shade for a layer of woodland flora beneath and also give structure to the design throughout the year.

Working with Architecture and the Landscape

Meadows and intermingling planting are often created as areas of transition between the garden and the 'natural' landscape beyond. This link can be heightened with the use of native plants common to the surrounding countryside or with the creation of shapes and forms within the design to echo those beyond the boundary of the garden. Tom Stuart-Smith's 'lollipop' trees are highly controlled garden forms that mirror the ancient deciduous trees in the distance (Plate 45). Keith Wiley also chooses plants that, although not necessarily native, have features in common with local plants. The underlying topography of the garden is sculpted to nestle into the landscape. Paths wind up and down and across the hillside and a dramatic vista opens to the valley beneath and the distant church spire (Plate 44).

Traditionally planting has been used to break up the hard lines of architecture or even to screen it completely. Yet naturalistic planting must be used with care next to the house. The issue of untidiness, especially in the damp, winter months, is of utmost importance as are the expectations of the client. Naturalistic schemes can be sited to great effect next to modernist architecture, where unfussy, simple lines and minimal colour schemes contrast with the intricacy of the planting (Plate 46). Evergreen grasses or perennials with interesting flowerheads are commonly used as they keep their form and colour over the winter months. Such designs are often characterized by sparse drifts or planes using a restricted plant palette.

It is the simplicity of Modernist architecture which acts as a foil to the small details of such planting schemes. When contrasted with more ornate brickwork the planting becomes lost and indistinct.

Creating the Middle Ground

The lack of winter interest is a criticism often levelled at naturalistic planting in a maritime climate. Many of the designers whose work is discussed on these pages introduce elements within their designs to counteract this difficulty. They range from clipped hedging, lollipop, pyramidal and buttress-shaped topiary, low box edging and coppiced trees, through architectural forms such as rocks, boulders, walls and benches, to sculpture. All work on the idea of contrast: clipped juxtaposed with wispy, hard with soft, vertical with horizontal, art with nature.

Creating Spaces

The dynamism of naturalistic planting encourages a fluid approach to the creation of paths and clearings; mown walkways can open to create seating spaces and narrow again to give an element of surprise or anticipation.

The design may call for geometric or organic grass paths through a random meadow (Plate 23) or an intermingling prairie, or merely for amorphous 'stepping gaps' amongst drifts in gravel or shingle (Plate 50). For a defined walk, crisp paving or decking walkways lead through the blocks and planes of planting.

Nigel Dunnett's work in deprived areas of Sheffield entails a detailed understanding of the use of the space. Desire lines are considered, as is possible vandalism. By mounding earth on either side of pathways, the design discourages people from walking across the planting, and the occasional foray by dogs and small children causes little damage.

When considering ways into and through planting, the participatory nature of the naturalistic scheme is most evident and this is where the designer must not fail. The visitor must be brought into the garden to experience it from all sides. It is not enough to stand on the edge and look in as with more traditional schemes. In the naturalistic scheme the experience is multi-layered. First is the overall view – the backdrop, the contrast with landscape or architecture. Then the anticipation is heightened perhaps by the rhythm of repeating blocks of colour or the drifts of flowing planting. The pathways into the garden encourage the visitor to explore, on a minute level, the planting and the tensions within.

PRACTITIONER PROFILE

BRITA VON SCHOENAICH AND TIM REES

Brita von Schoenaich and Tim Rees met whilst studying for the Diploma in Horticulture at Kew Gardens, London, in 1991. The impetus to form their design practice, Schoenaich Rees Landscape Architects, was based on a strong horticultural knowledge and a desire to combine this with landscape design in both the private and public sectors. Von Schoenaich's interest in naturalistic planting stems from her upbringing in Germany, and in 1994 she organized the first Perennial Perspectives Conference, bringing together designers to discuss the continental planting styles.

In Germany we are taught to consider first the habitat of the plant before looking at form and colour.

Planting Philosophy
Schoenaich Rees are interested in pushing the boundaries of planting design and are keen to experiment with new planting ideas. They have created annual and perennial meadows and have successfully naturalized perennials into grass.

They are working on combinations of perennials to create bedding schemes in public spaces using plants with naturalistic qualities and creating a natural rhythm within the planting. Schemes are based on strong design concepts and are designed to produce a succession of flowers and colours from spring to autumn.

Advice
- When planting perennials into grass, remove a 60cm square of turf, loosen soil and plant five perennials in 9cm pots for each 60cm square.
- Select cultivars which do not collapse in a wet winter.
- Work with a reduced number of species: 'less is more'.
- A concept within the naturalistic planting medium gives a discipline to the design.

Planting Combinations
Sow meadows in urban areas and city gardens with a combination of native and exotic species many of which flower later in the season after the natives are over. Use annuals such as *Escholzia californica*, *Linum rubrum*, *Papaver somniferum*.

Bedding Scheme for Tate Britain
- *Cosmos bipinnatus* 'Dazzler',
- *Crocosmia masoniorum*,
- *Foeniculum vulgare* 'Purpureum',
- *Lychnis coronaria*,
- *Nicotiana langsdorffii*,
- *Salvia farinacea* 'Victoria'.

Gardens open to the public
Ryton Organic Gardens.
Tate Britain, Bedding Schemes (Plates 51, 52).

Contact Details:
Schoenaich Rees Landscape Architects
149, Liverpool Road
London N1 0RF
Tel: 020 7837 3800
Fax: 020 7713 0191
Web: www.schoenaichrees.com

9 CONCLUSION AND THE WAY FORWARD

This book has analysed wild landscapes and provides examples of how to observe nature with design in mind. The techniques derived in Chapter 4 form a theoretical basis from which readers can develop their own naturalistic planting ethos. The choice varies from intermingling matrices to the more abstracted drifts, planes and blocks.

Practical applications to a maritime climate have been discussed in terms of problems that may be encountered. Solutions and options have been considered from the theoretical viewpoint and also from the experience of some practitioners working in the field.

It is clear that the difference between intensive and extensive maintenance is a crucial factor for the designer to consider; the maintenance requirements lead the design process.

As naturalism has developed over the twentieth and twenty-first centuries it has involved designers, gardeners and growers in research and experimentation. This process of education continues and will inevitably involve the public in the future. In existing plantings it has been found that the public's tolerance and appreciation of naturalistic schemes has been mainly positive, especially when they have an understanding of how it will develop.

At present designers are often limited by the availability of naturalistic varieties, and the influence of garden centres and the horticultural establishment will be factors in the development of this planting style.

An attractive factor in both private and public spaces is the low-maintenance possibilities of such schemes. Yet the specialist training of maintenance teams is crucial. An interesting development in Germany is the introduction of standard plant mixes available for public spaces. The mixes can be chosen according to the site conditions and are designed to achieve colourful and interesting effects when randomly planted. This negates the need for any designer input, and makes planting easy, but maintenance still requires selective weeding.

A thorough understanding of plant habitats and communities is essential for naturalistic design but also useful for more traditional schemes. Such knowledge can inform the selection of plants and combinations as well as their siting and planting densities. The increasing popularity of naturalistic perennials has led to concern over the issue of garden escapes. Plants that are well suited to the site conditions and able to seed freely may naturalize in to the surrounding landscape.

The experimental background of naturalism should lead designers to develop their observational skills and extrapolate their findings to create new planting combinations. A relinquishing of control over the garden will enable designers to observe changes in these designed plantings that may then inspire new ideas. The range of planting plans and illustrations in this book demonstrates the many ways in which designers are approaching naturalistic schemes, and designers should feel free to take their experimentation to the drawing board.

It is essential that designers continue the interdisciplinary debate with growers, horticulturists, ecologists and local planners on the applications of this planting – its advantages and limitations, its relationship to scale and architecture and its contribution to the design of garden space, both private and public.

Bibliography and Further Reading

Baines, C. & Smart, J. *A Guide to Habitat Creation*. London Ecology Unit/Packard, Chichester, 1991.

Bennett, J. *Wild About the Garden*. Macmillan, London, 1998.

Blanck, H. *Aspects of Change*. Alnarp, Sweden, 1996.

Brown, M. *Jardins des Champs*. Editions du Chêne, Paris, 1999.

Chatto, B. *Damp Garden* (revised edition). Cassell, London, 2005.

Chatto, B. *Gravel Garden*. Frances Lincoln, London, 2000.

Chatto, B. *Woodland Garden*. Cassell, London, 2002.

Clément, G. *Les Libres Jardins de Gilles Clément*. Editions du Chêne, Paris, 1999.

Clément, G. *Le Jardin en Mouvement*. Sens & Tonka, Paris (revised biennially).

Darke, R. *The American Woodland Garden*. Timber Press, Portland, Oregon, 2002.

Darke, R. *Color Encyclopaedia of Ornamental Grasses*. Timber Press, Portland, Oregon, 1999.

Druse, K. with Roach, M. *The Natural Habitat Garden*. Clarkson Potter, New York, 1994; paperback ed. Timber Press, Portland, Oregon, 2004.

Dunnett, N. & Hitchmough, J. *The Dynamic Landscape: Design, Ecology and Management of Naturalistic Urban Planting*. Spon Press, London, 2004.

Dutton, G. *Some Branch Against the Sky*. David & Charles, Newton Abbot, 1997.

Greenoak, F. *The Natural Garden*. Mitchell Beazley, London, 1998.

Grounds, R. *Plantfinder's Guide to Ornamental Grasses*. David & Charles, Newton Abbot, 1998.

Hansen, R. & Stahl, F. *Perennials and Their Garden Habitats*. Cambridge University Press, 1993.

Hinkley, D. *The Explorer's Garden*. Timber Press, Portland, Oregon, 1999.

Jarman, D. *Derek Jarman's Garden*. Thames and Hudson, London, 1995.

King, M. & Oudolf, P. *Gardening with Grasses*. Frances Lincoln, *London, 1998.*

Kingsbury, N. *Natural Gardening in Small Spaces*. Frances Lincoln, London, 2003.

Kingsbury, N. *The New Perennial Garden*. Frances Lincoln, London, 1996.

Landlife, *Wildflowers Work*, revised ed. Landlife, Liverpool, 2004.

Leopold, R. *Perennial Preview*. Perennial Plant Foundation, The Netherlands, 1997.

Lloyd, C. *Meadows*. Cassell, London, 2004.

Mabey, R. *Flora Britannica*. Sinclair-Stevenson, London, 1996.

Oehme, W. & Van Sweden, J. with Rademacher Frey, S. *Bold Romantic Gardens*. Acropolis Books, Reston, Virginia, 1990.

Oudolf, P. with Kingsbury, N. *Designing with Plants*. Conran Octopus, London, 1999.

Owen, J. *The Ecology of a Garden*. Cambridge University Press, 1991.

Pearson, D. *The Garden: A Year at Home Farm*. Ebury Press, London, 2001.

Phillips, R. *Wild Flowers of Britain*. Pan Books, London, 1978.

Phillips, R. & Rix, M. *Perennials,* vols 1 & 2. Macmillan, London, 1994.

Stevens, J. *The National Trust Book of Wild Flower Gardening*. Dorling Kindersley, London, 1990.

Thompson, P. *The Self-Sustaining Garden*. Batsford, London, 1997.

Trulove, J. *Designed Landscape Forum*. Spacemaker Press, Washington, DC, 1998.

Annual publications:

Daily Telegraph Good Garden Guide, King, P. & Lambert, K. Eds. Frances Lincoln, London.

RHS Garden Finder. Dorling Kindersley, London.

RHS Plant Finder. Dorling Kindersley, London.

Appendix – Summary of Practical Points

Issues	Advice
Grass weeds	Introduce *Rhinanthus minor* (yellow rattle) in sown meadows – it is an hemi-parasite and prefers grasses.[1] Note: often difficult to establish, so seek specialist advice.
High density planting	This is more successful if the plants are of similar competitiveness. Plants at higher densities do not grow so tall and are therefore less likely to flop. Less bare earth means less weed growth.
Perennial weeds and weed growth from the soil seed bank	Plant in high density groups to avoid bare earth while plants are establishing. Plant annual seed mixes between perennials for first year. Avoid disturbance of the soil as this will encourage weed germination. Use an inorganic mulch such as sand.[2] Remove all perennial weeds before planting. Plant in layers with a ground cover to suppress weed growth.
Site fertility	Reduce fertility when planting a perennial meadow. In a more fertile situation plant an annual meadow. Keep fertility low to reduce competition from grasses and to reduce height of perennials.
Slug predation	Cut back perennials in late winter rather than in spring to reduce predation.[3] Use slug pellets/nematodes until plants are established. One application of slug pellets is almost as effective as continuous applications.[4] Select plant varieties which are more resistant to slugs when established.

Issues	Advice
Wet or soggy plants in autumn	Select lower-growing cultivars which do not flop. Cut back unsightly perennials in autumn, leaving grasses until spring. Provide evergreens/grasses to give winter interest. Mulch with gravel for winter interest and to improve drainage.

[1] Dunnett, N. and Hitchmough, J. Conference at the University of Sheffield, January 2003. Research with Duncan Westbury.
[2] Dunnett, N. and Hitchmough, J. 'First in, last out.' *The Garden,* March 2001.
[3] Dunnett, N. and Hitchmough, J. Conference at the University of Sheffield, January 2003.
[4] Dunnett, N. and Hitchmough, J. 'First in, last out.' *The Garden,* March 2001.

Glossary

Biodiversity The existence of a wide variety of plant and animal species living in their natural environment.

Biotope planting A plant community resembling a natural habitat but with a mix of species chosen for both aesthetic and ecological reasons. It may include both native and exotic species.

Border perennial An exotic, hybridized and demanding plant requiring high maintenance and no competition.

Competitor A vigorous and large-growing species, especially on fertile soil or with the addition of nutrients.

Coppicing A traditional process designed to increase the yield of harvested wood resulting in a diverse woodland-edge community of herbaceous plants and bulbs happy in semi-shade.

Cultivar A group (or one among such a group) of cultivated plants clearly distinguished by one or more characteristics and which retains these characteristics when propagated; a distinct variety or race of plants that originated and persists under cultivation.

Dynamism The constant change and flux observable in 'natural' plantings, either through the seasons or over the years.

Ecology The study of the relationships of living organisms to their surroundings.

Ecosystem Plants and animals living together as a community and interacting with the physical environment. Any change to one may affect all in the system.

Emergent plant A plant which emerges from a lower plane of planting.

Environmental movement Those with a concern to preserve and protect the environment or natural world.

Ephemeral planting Plants which have, or give the impression of having, self-seeded.

Exotic Non-native plants.

Extensive maintenance Maintenance carried out to the whole planting area *en masse*, e.g. cutting back a meadow.

Frost pocket A small area subject to frost, which may damage tender plants. As cold air moves down a slope, it may meet an obstacle and settle, causing the air temperature to be lower than above.

Glyphosate A systemic weedkiller, which deactivates on contact with the soil.

Habitat The locality in which a plant naturally grows.

Heem Park Dutch ecological parks created in urban neighbourhoods with the intention of bringing nature to the towns and suburbs.

Hemi-parasite An organism that can survive independently of its host in certain conditions, or at certain stages of its life-cycle.

Horticulture The art or science of cultivating a garden.

Intensive maintenance Maintenance carried out on a specific part of a planting or an individual plant, e.g weeding out of grass seedlings.

Longevity The life of a plant, its method of growth and of reproduction.

Matrix Layers of vegetation making up an intermingling planting scheme – including roots below the surface, mat-forming plants and taller perennials.

Microclimate	A small, local climate within a larger climate area, such as a greenhouse or sheltered area of the garden.
Modernism	An early twentieth century movement in the arts, which turned away from traditional subject areas and means of expression, using artistic form and language to express intellectual and emotional states of mind.[1]
Native	A plant which occurs naturally in its country of use.
Nature conservation	The systematic protection and preservation of the environment; the careful management of natural resources and the environment.
Nematode	An organism used for parasitic control of slugs and pests.
Organic	Without the use of chemical fertilizers and pesticides.
Phenology	The growth habits and flowering pattern of a plant over the year.
Plant community	A group of plants growing naturally together.
Pointilliste	Characterized by dots of colour to create an image, e.g the paintings of Georges Seurat.
Ruderal	A vigorous species which takes advantage of transient conditions but is short-lived, reproducing successfully by seed.
Scarifications	Superficial scratches or scars to loosen the surface of the soil.
Self-seeding	The natural dispersion of seeds.
Soil seed bank	The dormant weed seeds in topsoil (approx. the top 100 mm) which will germinate whenever the soil is disturbed.
Static	Not moving; remaining in the original block or clump of planting.

Stress tolerator	A slow-growing species which does not respond to the addition of nutrients as strongly as a competitor (see above), occurring naturally in habitats where resources are limited.
Successional planting	Ensuring a succession of plants by intermingling species such that they grow up and give way to each other through the year.
Sustainable environment	An environment that both meets the needs of the present generation and does not compromise adversely those of future generations; sustainability is concerned with resource management.
Traditional processes	Horticultural and agricultural methods that have been developed over the centuries, and the response of plants to them.
Transient species	Species which emerge and then die back quickly leaving seeds to germinate when conditions are favourable (see ruderals).
Wild perennial	A less hybridized plant (see border perennnial), able to withstand the pressures of competition.

---

[1] Collins *Plain English Dictionary*.

GARDENS TO VISIT

Check for opening times
Naturalistic planting can be seen in the following gardens. Where appropriate, designers are shown in brackets.

Althorp House (Dan Pearson)
Althorp
Northampton
NN7 4HQ
Tel : 01604 770107

The Barn (Tom Stuart-Smith)
Serge Hill
Bedmond
St. Albans
(open under National Garden Scheme)

Beth Chatto's Garden
Elmstead Market
Colchester
CO7 7DB
Tel : 01206 822007

The Bloedel Reserve
7571 Northeast Dolphin Drive
Bainbridge Island
WA 98110
U.S.A.

Cowley Manor Hotel (Noël Kingsbury)
Cowley
Gloucestershire
Tel : 01242 870900

Denmans Garden (John Brookes)
Fontwell
Arundel
BN18 0SU
Tel : 01243 542808

Derek Jarman's garden (visitors welcome, but please do not disturb occupant)
Dungeness
Kent

Fairleigh Gateway (Nigel Dunnett)
Manor Estate
Sheffield

The Garden House (Keith Wiley)
Buckland Monachorum
Yelverton
Devon
PL20 7LQ
Tel : 01822 854769

The Garden House (Lee Heykoop)
42 Wragby Road
Bardney
Lincs
LN3 5XL
Tel: 01526 397307

Great Dixter (Christopher Lloyd)
Dixter Road
Northiam
Rye
TN31 6PH
Tel : 01797 252878

Jac. P. Thijssepark (C.P. Broerse)
Prins Bernhardlaan
Amstelveen
Netherlands

Kwekerij Oudolf (Piet Oudolf)
Broekstraat 17
6999 DE Hummelo
The Netherlands

Lady Farm (Judy Pearce and Mary Payne)
Chelwood
Bristol
BS18 4NN
Tel : 01761 490770

Parc André Citroën (Gilles Clément)
Paris 15
France

Pensthorpe Waterfowl Park (Piet Oudolf)
Pensthorpe
Fakenham
Norfolk
NR21 0LN
Tel : 01328 855905

Prionatuinen (Henk Gerritsen)
Schuineslootweg 13
7777 RE Schuinesloot
Netherlands
Tel: 0031 523 681734

RHS Garden at Hyde Hall
The Dry Garden
Buckhatch Lane
Rettenden
Chelmsford
Essex
CM3 8ET
Tel : 01245 400256

RHS Garden at Wisley (Piet Oudolf)
Wisley
Woking
Surrey
GU23 6QB
Tel : 01483 224234

Ryton Organic Gardens (Schoenaich Rees)
Ryton-on-Dunsmore
Coventry
CV8 3LG
Tel : 02476 303517

Scampston Hall (Piet Oudolf)
Scampston, Malton
North Yorkshire YO17 8NG
Tel: 01944 759111

Schau und Sichtungsgarten Hermannshof,
(Urs Walser)
Babostrasse 5
69469 Weinheim
Germany
Tel: 0049 6201 13652

Sheffield Botanical Gardens (Nigel Dunnett)
Sheffield
S10 2LN
Tel : 0114 267115

Sheffield General Cemetery (Nigel Dunnett)
Woodland Garden
Sheffield

Sticky Wicket (Mrs Pam Lewis)
Buckland Newton
Dorchester
Dorset
DT2 7BY
Tel : 01300 345476

Tate Britain (Schoenaich Rees)
Millbank
London
SW1P 4RG

Waltham Place (Henk Gerritsen)
White Waltham
Maidenhead
SL6 3JH
Tel: 01628 825517

Webbs of Wychbold (Noël Kingsbury)
Wychbold
Droitwich Spa
Worcestershire
WR9 0DG
Tel : 01527 860000

Westpark (Rosemarie Weisse)
80539 München
Germany

Yalding Organic Gardens
Benover Road
Yalding
Maidstone
Kent
ME18 6EX
Tel : 01622 814650

Plant List

Acanthus spinosus 21
Acer palmatum Pl.42
Achillea
  – 'Apfelblüte' 21
  – 'Fanal' 24, Pl.31
  – 'Feuerland' 20, 21
  – *grandifolia* 10, Pl.10
  – *millefolium* (yarrow) 18
  – 'Moonshine' 23, 24
  – 'Summerwine' 21
  – *umbellata* 'Walther 'Funcke' 21
Allium
  – *cristophii* 21
  – *moly* 24
  – *sphaerocephalon* Pl.4
  – *ursinum* 19
Amelanchier lamarckii 19
Ammophila arenaria (marram grass) 13, Pl.16
Amsonia tabernaemontana var. *salicifolia* 26, 27
Anemone
  – *nemorosa* 19
  – *x hybrida* 8
annuals Pl.11
Aquilegia vulgaris 9, 10
Artemisia
  – *alba* 'Canescens' 23, 24
  – *ludoviciana* 'Silver Queen' 23
  – 'Powis Castle' 25
Arum italicum 19
Asphodeline liburnica 21, 25
Aster
  – *divaricatus* 19
  – *ericoides* cvs. 17

  – *x frikartii* 'Monch' 21, 25
  – *laevis* 'Climax' 6
  – 'Little Carlow' 6
  – *novi belgii* 22
  – species 17, 22
  – *turbinellus* 6, 17, 21
Astilbe chinensis var. *taquettii* 'Purpurlanze' 26, 27, Pls.33, 34

Baptisia australis 17, 21
Berberis thunbergii f. *atropurpurea* 'Atropurpurea Nana' 24
bluebell *see Hyacinthoides non-scripta*
Boltonia asteroides var. *latisquama* 20, 21
Bromus ramosus 19

Calamagrostis
  – *x acutiflora* 'Karl Foerster' 6, 10, 24, Pls.22, 30, 48
  – *brachytricha* 21, Pl.26
Californian poppy *see Eschscholzia californica*
Camassia quamash 17
Campanula lactiflora 10, Pls.10, 12
campion *see Silene dioica*
Carex
  – *comans* 6, (bronze form) 24
  – *flagellifera* 24
  – *pendula* Pl.42
  – *nigra* (lesser knapweed) 18
Carpinus betulus (hornbeam) Pl.32
Centaurea
  – *cyanus* (cornflower) Pl.11
  – *benoistii* 21
  – *nigra* (lesser knapweed) 18

Centranthus ruber Pl.50
Cercidiphyllum japonicum Pl.42
Chaerophyllum hirsutum 27
Cimicifuga ramosa Pl.21
Coreopsis verticillata 23, 24
cornflower *see Centaurea cyanus*
Cornus cousa var. *chinensis* Pl.40
Corylus avellana (hazel) 19, Pl.24
Cosmos bipinnatus 'Dazzler' 34, Pl.52
Crambe
  – *cordifolia* 13
  – *maritima* Pl.50
Crocosmia
  – 'Lucifer' Pl.37
  – *masoniorum* 34

Dactylorhiza fuchsii (common spotted orchid) 18
Daucus carota (wild carrot) 18
Deschampsia cespitosa 'Goldtau' 26, 27, Pl.33
Dianthus carthusianum 25
Dierama pulcherrimum Pl.36
Digitalis
  – *ferruginea* 19, Pl.35
  – *purpurea* Pl.3

Echinacea purpurea 17
  – 'Leuchstern' 21
  – 'Robert Bloom' 21
Eryngium
  – *agavifolium* Pl.36
  – *alpinum* 'Blue Star' 21
  – *amethystinum* 21
  – *bourgatii* 23, 24, 25

– *giganteum* 9, Pls.4, 5
– *x tripartitum* 21
Eschscholzia californica (Californian poppy) 13, Pl.11
Eucalyptus species 20
Eupatorium
   – *fistulosum* 'Atropurpureum' 17
   – species Pl.21
Euphorbia
   – *amygdaloides* var. *robbiae* 8
   – *griffithii* 'Dixter' 21, 26, 27
   – *myrsinites* 24
   – *palustris* 6
   – *polychroma* 24

ferns Pl.18
Festuca
   – *amethystina* 23, Pl.32
   – *mairei* 26, 27
Filipendula ulmaria 17
Foeniculum vulgare 'Purpureum' 28, 34
forget-me-not *see Myosotis*
Fraxinus excelsior (ash) 19

Galium
   – *mollugo* (hedge bedstraw) 19
   – *odoratum* (woodruff) 9, 19
   – *verum* (lady's bedstraw) 18
Genista tinctoria (dyer's greenwood) 18
Geranium
   – 'Ann Folkard' 21
   – 'Johnson's Blue' 6
   – *macrorrhizum* 9
   – *x oxonianum* cvs 6
   – 'Rebecca Moss' 27

– 'Patricia' Pl.37
– *phaeum* 17, 27
– *pratense* (meadow cranesbill) 18
– *psilostemon* 10, 19, Pl.12
– *sanguineum* 27
– species 26, Pl.22
– *sylvaticum* 10, 17, 19
grasses, ornamental 6, 10, 24, 30, Pls.4, 7, 9, 20, 21, 22, 24, 25, 26, 27, 28, 30, 31, 32, 33, 35, 41, 42, 48

hazel Pl.24
Helenium 'Rubinzwerg' 21, Pl.26
   – species Pl.2
Helianthus 'Lemon Queen' 6, 10, Pl.7
Helleborus
   – *foetidus* 10, Pl.12
   – *orientalis* 8
Hemerocallis
   – 'Golden chimes' 21
   – 'Mrs Hugh Johnson' 21
   – 'Stafford' Pl.37
Hesperis matronalis (sweet rocket) 19, Pl.40
honesty *see Lunaria annua*
hornbeam *see Carpinus betulus*
Hyacinthoides non-scripta (bluebell) 19, Pl.13
Hypericum perforatum (common St John's wort) 18

Iris sibirica Pl.40

Kniphophia species 23, 24, 25, Pls.9, 30

Lamium

– *galeobdolon* 9
– *orvata* 27
Leontodon hispidus (rough hawkbit) 18
Leucanthemum vulgare (oxeye daisy) 18
Liatris spicata 17
Linaria vulgaris (common toadflax) Pl.11
Lindelofia longiflora 21
Lotus
   – *corniculatus* (common bird's foot trefoil) 18
   – *uliginosus* (syn. *pedunculatus*)(greater bird's foot trefoil) 18
Lunaria annua (honesty) 9, 19
Lychnis coronaria 34, Pl.52
   – Alba group Pl.46
   – *flos-cuculi* (ragged robin) 18
Lythrum
   – *salicaria* 10, 17, Pl.6
   – *virgatum* 26, 27

Macleaya cordata 17
Malva moschata (musk mallow) 18
marram grass *see Ammophila arenaria*
Matteucia struthiopteris 10
Melica uniflora 19, Pl.42
Medicago sativa (lucerne) 18
Milium effusum (wood millet) 19
Miscanthus sinensis 6, 22, Pl.7
   – species 22, 24, 28
Molinia caerulea 26, 27
   – 'Transparent' 28
Monarda
   – cultivars 17, Pl.2
   – 'Mohawk' 27
   – 'Präirienacht' 21
Myosotis species 9

Narcissus poeticus (pheasant's eye) 19
 – *poeticus* var. *recurvus* 19
native plants 1, 7, Pl.24
Nepeta
 – *racemosa* 'Walker's Low' 25
 – *sibirica* 21
Nicotiana langsdorfii 34

Oenothera macrocarpa 24
Origanum pulchellum 'Rosenkuppel' 26, 27

Panicum virgatum 17
 – 'Rehbraun' 20, 21, 26, 27
 – 'Rotstralbusch' 20, 21
 – 'Strictum' 26, 27
Papaver rhoeas (Shirley poppy) Pl.11
Persicaria
 – *amplexicaulis* cvs. 17, 19, Pl.6
 – 'Firedance' 26, 27
 – 'Rosea' 26, 27
 – *bistorta* 'Superba' 6
Phlox maculata 'Delta' 26, 27
Pimpinella saxifraga (burnet saxifrage) 18
Plantago lanceolata (ribwort plantain) 18
poppies *see* Papaver, Eschcholzia
Primula
 – *elatior* (oxslip) Pl.1
 – *veris* (cowslip) 18
 – *vulgaris* (primrose) 10, 19
Prunella vulgaris (self-heal) 18

Rannculus
 – *acris* (meadow buttercup) 18, 19
 – *ficaria* (lesser celandine) 19
reeds Pl.19

Rhinanthus minor (yellow rattle) 37
Rhus typhina 19, Pl.25
ruderal plants 8, 9, *see* glossary
Rudbeckia fulgida var. *deamii* 6, 17, 19, Pl.25
Rumex acetosa (common sorrel) 18

Salvia
 – *farinacea* 'Victoria' 34
 – *nemorosa* 'Ostfriesland' 21
 – *officinalis* 'Würzburg' 26, 27
 – x *sylvestris* 'Blauhügel' 21, 25, Pl.32
 – *xs.* 'Mainacht' 21, 24, Pl.31
 – var. *turkestanica* 21
 – *verticillata* 'Purple Rain' 26, 27
Sanguisorba
 – *menziesii* 26, 27
 – 'Tanna' 26, 27, Pl.36
Santolina species 28
Saponaria x lempergii 'Max Frei' 26, 27
Scabiosa japonica var. *alpina* 26, 27
Scutellaria incana 21, 26, 27
Sedum
 – *spectabile* 9
 – *telephium* 'Matrona' 25
 – *tenuifolia* 17
Sesleria nitida 26, 27
Shirley poppy *see Papaver rhoeas*
Silene dioica (red campion) 18, 19
Sisyrinchium striatum Pl.2
Solidago
 – *rigida* 17
 – *rugosa* 'Fireworks' 6
Solidaster luteus 'Lemore' 21
Sorghastrum avenaceum (syn.*nutans*) 'Indian
 Steel' 17

Stachys
 – *byzantina* 'Silver Carpet' 25
 – *macrantha* 'Superba' 26, 27
 – *monieri* 'Hummelo' 26, 27
 – *officinalis* (betony) 18
Stipa
 – *arundinacea* 6, 9, 20, 21
 – *barbata* Pl.35
 – *calamagrostis* 20, 21, Pl.26
 – *gigantea* 21, 24
 – *offneri* 26, 27
 – *tenuissima* 20, 23, 24, Pls.4, 30, 41
 – *turkestanica* 26, 27
Succisa pratensis (devil's bit scabious) 18

Tanacetum vulgare (tansy) Pl.11
Taxus baccata (yew) Pl.32
 – hedges Pl.2
Tellima grandiflora Pl.40
Thalictrum aquilegifolium 26, 27
Trifolium pratense (red clover) 18
Tulipa tarda 24

Valeriana officinalis 17
Verbascum olympicum 23, 24, Pl.30
Verbena
 – *bonariensis* 21, 22, 28
 – *hastata* 17
Veronica spicata 'Spitzentraum' 26, 27
Veronicastrum virginicum
 – 'Fascination' 26, 27, Pls.34, 35
 – 'Temptation' 26, 27
Viola odoratum (violet) 19

yew *see Taxus baccata* 23

Index